Yorkshire Humour

W.R. Mitchell, a native of Skipton, 'Gateway to the Yorkshire Dales', began a journalistic career on the *Craven Herald and Pioneer* during the Second World War, and then started work on *The Dalesman* magazine, an association which lasted forty years. Bill Mitchell was also responsible for editing *Cumbria* magazine. During this time, he wrote many books about history, topography and wildlife in Northern England and Scotland. He also made a collection of humorous tales, which he has used in countless talks.

Since 'retiring' in 1988 he has followed his interests as an author, lecturer and naturalist, having a special love for the hill country and its people. He is the author of over a hundred books.

> A level-headed Yorkshireman is
> one with a chip on each shoulder.

Yorkshire Humour

W.R. MITCHELL

ROBERT HALE · LONDON

ISBN 0 7090 5831 4

Robert Hale Limited
Clerkenwell House
Clerkenwell Green
London EC1R 0HT

·   2   4   6   8   10   9   7   5   3   1

Photoset in North Wales by
Derek Doyle & Associates, Mold, Clwyd.
Printed in Great Britain by
St Edmundsbury Press Ltd, Bury St Edmunds, Suffolk.
Bound by WBC Book Manufacturers Limited,
Bridgend, Mid-Glamorgan.

Contents

for PAM DOUGLAS
(a naturalised Yorkshirewoman)

Acknowledgements

The author wishes to thank the Epworth Press for permission to use an extract from *Yorkshire Wit and Humour* by H.L. Gee. Thanks are also due to Mark W. Jones for the extract from his book *Snicklegates*.

1 A Funny County

See all, hear all, say nowt;
Eit all, sup all, pay nowt,
And if tha ivver does owt fer nowt
Allus do it for thissen

This Yorkshire commandment is typical of the music-hall humour in Great-grandfather's day, when we were in a self-mocking phase and dialect verse was in the vogue. You'll find the commandment printed on T-shirts, souvenir mugs and postcards. For all I know it may be inscribed in stone, among the names of civic dignitaries, on a West Riding town hall.

Yorkshire folk are not mean, of course. Just careful wi' money, which is generally referred to as 'brass'. An old lady who kept her money in a tin box, when advised to bank it because she was losing the interest, replied: 'I put a bit extra in t'tin for interest every week.' A Dales farmer with a reputation for meanness went by horse and trap to Skipton on market-day and, having a hair lodged in one eye, he called at the smithy in Grassington Road to get it removed. The smith obliged, then – knowing of the farmer's frugal ways – said: 'Ista bahn to take that hair now or collect it later?'

It might have been the same farmer who, soon after the arrival of his first baby, sneaked into the child's bedroom. His wife found him standing by the cot and gazing intently into it. Touched by the sight, she put her arms around him. Tears welled up in her eyes. She asked her husband what he was thinking about. He said: 'Nay, lass – I think we paid far too much for that cot.'

Farmers are not inclined to 'throw brass abaht'. The son of a Dales farmer went into a far country for a while and then returned unexpectedly, reminding his father of the parable of the prodigal son. A friend said: 'I suppose he killed t'fatted calf for thee.'

The farmer's son said: 'Nay, lad – he didn't kill t'fatted calf but he damn near killed t'prodigal son.'

The woolmen of West Yorkshire are rarely off duty, even when taking the family to the annual nativity play at the local church. One of the textile brethren who listened to children singing the carol *While Shepherds Watched* remarked to his neighbour: 'I reckon they were wise to watch yon sheep now that t'price o' wool's gone up.' When, years ago, high prices prevailed at the Australian wool sales, a Bradford wool-buyer cabled to his firm: 'Bought 500 bales. Feather in my cap.' On the second day, the message was repeated and when the third day came the cable contained the message: 'Bought 1,000 bales. Third feather in my cap.'

The cabled reply from Bradford was brief and to the point: 'Firm bankrupt. Use feathers to fly home.'

It is 'Yorksher' to borrow rather than buy. When a Leeds man was asked by a friend if he had a tin of red paint he could use to fettle up some woodwork, the immediate response was: 'Aye, lad – pop round for it tomorn.' (This friend would soon need to borrow his pal's lawnmower). The friend did 'pop' round and was met by a sorrowful wife, who told him her husband had just died. 'E, I'm right sorry to hear that, love,' was the immediate response. He paused for a few seconds and added: 'Had he time to say owt about a tin o' red paint?' It was undoubtedly the same man who greeted any visitor to the house with the words: 'If tha's getten owt to take, ah'll tek it. If tha's wanting some brass, see t'wife!'

We lay on our gormlessness for the benefit of visitors. It gives us an edge over our business rivals, who think they are about to score over us and find out later they've been 'plucked' once again. I've seen some gormless farmers at auction marts but realised that behind the bland expression has been a mind as sharp as a computer. And, as Norman Thornber, a Dales corn merchant, used to tell me: 'If you act like a know-it-all, you learn nowt.'

Yorkshire folk are like the Scots – very clannish, though we don't go to the extent of wearing kilts, being careful not to 'cast a clout till May be out'. (That old saying applies to the hawthorn tree, which is called the may but doesn't put on its best show of blossom till early June. So be careful over clout-casting.) Yorkshirewomen like to wear summat plain. They had a liking for bustles and flounces till a hard-up mill-town lass set a new style when she told her dressmaker: 'I want summat plain – not puckered up at t'backside.'

A sociologist would attribute the Yorkshireman's general manner, dour, phlegmatic, blunt, even rude, to the privations of the industrial past – the trouble at t'mill period when there were a few bosses and an army of workers, the last-named being worked to death and paid next to nowt. Retirement was a moment of time between leaving work and entering the cemetery. The sociologist might be reminded that milldom represents less than ten per cent of Yorkshire as a whole. Why, I could take you northwards from Skipton to the Scottish border and you wouldn't see a mill chimney on the way.

John Braine's novel, *Room at the Top*, dealt with social aspiration and the possibility of an ordinary working-class lad rising to the heights, in this case through some sly moves, including marrying the boss's daughter – the quick route to promotion which was followed by many others. It was to be a story of our (mercenary) times. Braine did give an authentic West Riding background and some believable Yorkshire characters. But I remember the chill which passed through the primmer folk in the county when this book was published. It was denounced as pornography.

Nowadays it would not raise an eyebrow. You may have heard the story of a Yorkshireman who said to his pal: 'What about all this pornography?'

His friend replied: 'Nay, lad, I don't know owt about it. I haven't got a pornograph.'

Wilfred Pickles, a Halifax lad, rose to fame on t'wireless without forfeiting his Yorkshireness, nor resorting to mucky tales. Wilfred was amused by the Yorkshireman's capacity for understatement. He also mentioned the caution shown in business dealings, when he gives the impression of impending doom. 'Be good,' they exort each other on parting, 'behave thiself'.

My favourite Wilfred Pickles tale is of the working-class family who travelled from the West Riding to Blackpool in Wakes Week, the annual holidaytime, when – whilst walking along the promenade – you might meet up with countless friends and neighbours. It was one occasion when you might show off. And you were always anxious to act 'proper' and not be shown up.

The family mentioned by Wilfred were in the dining room when the small son said: 'Muum-mm' in such a way she knew instantly he wanted to go to the toilet.

To avoid embarrassment, she whispered: 'It's upstairs, luv. Next door to t'bathroom.' The lad slipped away. Minutes later, his voice – as loud and intense as a mill buzzer – drifted down several flights of steps. The mother just had to respond. 'What, luv?' she shouted.

The small boy yelled: 'I can see Blackpool Tower when I'm on t'closet.'

We Yorkshire folk feel a bit uneasy when we go into distant parts – like Lancashire. For hundreds of years, we've lived cosily behind our border. The biggest shock to Yorkshire pride was 1974, when the bureaucrats, using our hard-earned brass, mucked about with the Yorkshire boundaries. They said that they could save us a lot of money by making the counties look neat and tidy. It turned out to be an expensive rehearsal for the Community Charge.

Yorkshire is England's greatest county, judging by its size. An American stationed among the radomes on Menwith Hill, near Harrogate, told me: 'Yorkshire seems to be the Texas of England. It's big. And you sure do brag about it.' He was right. I might take the analogy a little further. Just as America consists of states with cultural variety, but with a strong national identity, so Yorkshire is made up of at least a dozen mini-regions. Pick a middle-aged or elderly person from each region, bring them together, and you'd be capped (astonished) at differences in speech and attitude. Each, however, would be bursting with county pride.

The Boundary Commission, reshaping the bounds of local government, needlessly filleted Yorkshire, handing out chunks to adjacent counties and creating, in the place of the East Riding, an administrative area known as North Humberside. When a farmer living in the far west was asked for his views on a transfer to Lancashire, he simply replied: 'I couldn't stand t'climate.' In the event, he was allowed to remain in Yorkshire.

Whitehall, a thorn in the flesh of Yorkshire for centuries, is now trying to throw the process (expensively) into reverse. Meanwhile, it stirred up Yorkshire pride. Someone started the Yorkshire Society, which organised Yorkshire Day (1 August), gathering together civic dignitaries who process to a church service. The society is keen to emphasise the ancient Ridings which, as far as I know, still exist, though they have been overlaid by the new local government areas.

Yorkshire Day is well-supported, not least by the media, though it's surprising how many converted Lancashire men are proclaiming the greatness of the county. Yorkshireness is being stretched almost as much as Aunt Mabel's corsets. You no longer have to be born in Yorkshire to belong to a Yorkshire society, nor indeed to play cricket for Yorkshire. An Irish-born bishop preached at a Yorkshire Day service in my home town of Skipton. Off-comers have infiltrated many Yorkshire organisations. Now there's a rush of refugees from the south-west to share in the good life between Tees and Trent.

Yorkshire's tail wags most furiously at the border crossings, such as that between Foulridge and Kelbrook, where recently I saw a prominent notice featuring a white rose and the words 'Yorkshire Welcomes You'! At Hawes, I remind myself of the small-scale, economical local government of yesterday. The Council had a staff of three: a clerk, an engineer and a girl to do the clerical work and make the tea. It was, as I recall, good tea, for she pre-warmed the pot. The productivity of this trio of dedicated local government workers was astonishing, and they always managed to find time for face-to-face chats about specific problems.

Yorkshire's old familiar boast – that there are more acres in Yorkshire (3,923,359) than letters in the Bible (3,566,840) – is meaningless now that acres have been transformed into hectares. Anyway, how many people regularly read the Bible nowadays, much less go to the trouble of counting words? The vicar of a Yorkshire parish was delighted, when visiting an old countryman, to see him poring over the Old Testament. 'Nay, vicar, I'se just interested in names,' he said. 'My dog's had a litter o' pups and I've got to find names for each of 'em.'

Biblical names for people were commonplace. A distant relative of mine was christened Hobadiah but was usually referred to matily as 'our 'Ob'. The farmer-preachers of rural Methodism, whose everyday speech was laden with Biblical expressions from the book they read daily, had a particular love for the Old Testament stories, such as that about the prodigal son, who returned home after feeding swine. A Nidderdale preacher who invariably chose this theme said, dramatically, just before he closed his sermon: 'And soa t'lad came home agean. And he wor all clarted wi' pig muck.'

We Yorkshire folk have a realistic outlook, a consequence –

according to Ranulph Higden (a southerner), writing in the fourteenth century – of our hard lives. He added:

> ... Alle the languages of the Northumbres and specially at York is so sharp, slyting frotying and unshape that we sothern men may unneth understande that language. And also by cause that the kynges of England abyde and dwelle more in the south countrey than in the north country. The cause ... is that there is better corn londe more peple more noble cytees and more proufytable havens in the south country than in the north.

We're not at our best in crowds, unless it happens to be among the livestock at the Great Yorkshire Show, when the essence of Yorkshire life and activity is compressed on a tract of land near Harrogate. I took a farmer to the show. Impressed by the large attendance, I asked him to estimate the number of people present. He had spent an appreciable part of his working life counting sheep! After a while, the farmer said: 'Nay, I couldn't begin to count this lot. But if thou got 'em to run through yon gate-hole I'd soon tell thee.' He would hurriedly count them, two by two, and at every hundred slip a small pebble from one trouser pocket to the other – an ancient form of computer.

The sale rings of auction marts, such as Hawes or Skipton, can be thronged wi' folk. A story told of Hellifield auction (now, alas, closed) concerns two brothers who were cattle-dealers. If they could sell their stock surreptitiously, without the benefit of a professional auctioneer, and save on commission, then they would do so. One haggled over the price of a cow for so long, his brother sidled up beside him and whispered: 'Have ye bowt it?'

'Not yet.'

The brother said, anxiously: 'Well hurry up – I've just selt [sold] it.'

One brother was married and in due course his wife presented him with a son. The lad seemed to miss babyhood and was soon picking up farming ways and 'makkin' issen useful' about the place. He had a cloth cap worn (farming fashion) with the neb at one side. He accompanied his father to Hellifield auction but lacked father's patience when surreptitiously haggling over the price of a cow. After ten minutes, he sidled up to Dad and said, in an audible whisper: 'Get the bugger selled.'

You might reckon on a large crowd of Yorkshire folk at Headingley for a test match. For many, cricket has almost attained the status of a religion. A well-worn cricketing anecdote concerns Wilfred Rhodes and George Hirst. They had been set for victory over Middlesex at Lords one Saturday when the clouds massed and the rain fell. Little further play was possible that day. Rhodes and Hirst, out walking in blazing sunshine next day, discussed the match. Hirst considered that if the weather had been as good on the previous day, they would have had Middlesex out by half-past twelve. Rhodes corrected him. 'Nay, George – we'd have scuttled 'em out by a quarter to one.'

Freddie Trueman, OBE, used to visit Settle, in North Ribblesdale, with the Yorkshire team. He left the home wickets bruised and battered and once lifted a ball clean out of the field, across a garden and over a council house. It landed in Marshfield Road. Fred's magnificent hit was not the best recorded at Settle. One ball travelled seventy-two miles. (It landed in the carriage of a passing train and was discovered at Carlisle). Fred tells of a Nidderdale man who took the opportunity of going to a test match and paying his subscription to the club. The secretary said: 'Attendance is a bit disappointing.'

The visitor said: 'Don't worry – there'll be plenty this afternoon … It's half day closing in Patela [Pateley Bridge].'

One day I must tell Fred about the cricket match held in a rural area where the squire was given out l.b.w. He wasn't very pleased. Stopping on his way back to the pavilion, he had a word with the man in the white coat, telling him that having reached such a decision he needed some new glasses. The man in the white coat said: 'So do you, mate. I'm selling ice cream.'

God loves a good giver. He's not over-fond of a good taker. As I've already mentioned, we Yorkshire folk are careful with our brass. We don't chuck it about. It's taken a long time for us to addle (earn) it. The chapel folk had what they called a faith tea. Food brought by each person was pooled. It did at least allow people to taste the kitchen products – sandwiches, pastries or sponge cakes – of their friends. The name faith tea was changed when a man said to the steward: 'I've more faith than t'lot o' you; I've browt nowt.'

It's now called a Jacob's Join, an alliteration, and reminds me of the biblical story of Jacob and his vision of a ladder, stretching from earth to heaven, with angels ascending and descending. A teacher in a Dales school asked a farmer's son why this should be. The lad – with a full measure of Yorkshire realism, and fully aware that angels are equipped with wings – said: 'Appen they were in t'moult.'

T'chapel was an important element in Yorkshire rural life until quite recently. Even now, there are some chapels where, on special occasions, like anniversaries and harvest festivals, the seating is fully occupied. At Garsdale Head, within shouting distance of the Settle–Carlisle, a service planned for hikers (many of whom were to arrive by train from Settle) had to be delayed for an hour or so when the train was held up by a cow on the tracks. There was a tense moment when two burly motor-cyclists, wearing leather jackets, strode into the chapel. They looked intimidating, until one of them removed his leather jacket and revealed a jumper on which was emblazoned 'Association of Christian Bikers'.

The realistic attitude of many natives of Yorkshire is illustrated by a Wharfedale girl who disgraced her updale family by marrying a lad out of t'town. Eventually, the mother softened far enough to agree to visit the young couple and the new baby in their posh home at Skipton. She travelled from her centuries-old cottage, with its basic amenities, and eventually entered what the young folk considered to be their dream house, with its fitted cupboards and hot and cold water. There was even a washing machine, a surprise for an old lady who had always used a tub, posser and mangle. Said her daughter: 'What do you think of the place, Mum?'

Mum, determined (in the Dales way) not to like everything, said: 'How's ta going to get t'coffin down yon narrow stairs?'

Yorkshire is a kingdom within a kingdom. It is both broad and varied. The scenic variations are breathtaking, from the smooth-sided Howgill Fells, which have been compared to a herd of elephants which lay down to sleep, to the dazzling termination just north of Bridlington of the crescent of chalk which forms the Yorkshire Wolds. Or you might take another line, from the red-roofed fishing town of Whitby, in Captain Cook country, to Bonnie Bowland, where they used to have the outline of a chubby archer on medallions at the top of the road signs. Bowland was not a playground of Robin Hood. It was once a forest (meaning a chase for wild animals) but economically more important than sport was the venture of ranching cattle. Bolland is said to mean, unroman-tically, 'land of cattle'.

York, Beverley, Ripon and Selby have especially impressive

churches. Way out west, where the breezes ruffle t'cut (canal) and the air holds the sweet tang of wool grease, churches are outnumbered by chapels – box-like structures with Grecian façades and windows which break away from the squared-off mill type, being rounded at the top. It was said in the old West Riding that if you talked o' t'Devil you'd 'appen 'ear his clogs clattering. In the big, spired, soot-skimmed Victorian churches, the Devil was kept at bay by Mr Handel's oratorio the *Messiah* rendered by singers who got so het-up (excited) they made the window rattle.

Methodist parsons are thick on the ground when it's the turn of, say, Bradford to play host to conference. A farmer who saw a crowd of crow-black, white-collared men pouring on to the pavement at lunch-time said to his companion: 'Ah reckon parsons is like good muck – best spread out.' A cockney parson I knew in Craven introduced me when I agreed to talk to his Wesley Guild about the Yorkshire Dales. The minister gave the title as 'Toiles from the Doiles'.

The West Riding (of beloved memory) impressed the visitor by the size and weight of its principal buildings. Town halls brushed the clouds. Mills blocked out half the sky. Chimneys reached out for the sun. For some manufacturers, creating a new enterprise was in part an ego-trip. The Victorian who became Sir John Edward Wainhouse would have been forgotten but for his desire, in 1871, to build a chimney to carry away fumes from his dyeworks.

It was at a time when smoke abatement regulations had come into force, to prevent mill-owners filling the lungs of the populace with smoke and grit. Wainhouse had to build high, but his own plans did not reach fruition. It was left to his manager, Henry Mossman, to finish the enterprise. Henry did not wish to go to the considerable expense of completing the chimney, to conform with the Smoke Abatement Act, so Sir John kept the 275-foot structure, which he converted into an observation tower. Now a considerable novelty, it is open to the public several times a year.

When the Brontë lasses wrote their strange novels in the draughty parsonage at the edge of Haworth Moor, they were familiar with the lurid sights of the industrialised Aire Valley and doubtless, in their moorland tramping, picked up smuts of soot on their clothes. Charlotte wrote: 'Speak of the North – a lonely moor, silent and still and trackless lies …' The North York Moors outclass those of Haworth in quality and scale.

The moorland farmers have always been a group apart, while sharing such Yorkshire characteristics as thrift. A man asked a farmer if he could hire a horse. The farmer, in order to assess how much he would charge, said: 'How long will you want it?'

The enquirer, missing the point, said: 'As long as thou can manage, lad – there's three on us.'

Among the low-country villages, a special favourite is Coxwold, with its honeyed stone and picture-postcard type houses. Shandy Hall was between 1760 and 1768 the home of Laurence Sterne, parson and author of *Tristram Shandy*, the first modern novel, though the reader would not immediately associate the structure of today's novel with Sterne's collection of autobiographical jottings, scandalous anecdotes and romantic musings.

He lived a good life at Coxwold and was 'as happy as a prince'. He might 'sit down alone to venison, fish and wildfowl or a couple of ducks, with curds, strawberries and cream and all the simple plenty which a rich valley under the Hambleton Hills can produce'. He doubtless thanked the Lord in Latin. Another Coxwold man acknowledged a good meal by patting his capacious stomach and saying: 'Ay, good belly – I wish thou were empty agean.'

North of the Aire Gap is the largest outcrop of limestone in Britain, forming part of the Dales National Park. The gritstone of the Southern Pennines is at its darkest in the Brontë country of Haworth, to which reference has already been made. It is difficult to think of Haworth dispassionately. The residence of the Brontës, representing less than half a century of Haworth's long history, dominates all. For me, the Brontës have lost their charm under a torrent of research into the Brontë psyche by students who prefer the library to the open moor. Charm is a delicate thing which cannot survive a tidal wave of humanity – the estimated million visitors a year to the old hillside village.

Dr William Cartman, my great-great-grandfather, was a personal friend of Patrick Brontë and his daughter Charlotte. He'd preach a sermon from the top of a three-decker pulpit in the old Haworth Church and then pop into the parsonage for a cup o' tea and, perhaps a scone. Now t'owd parsonage is a-wash with humanity, though the attendance figure has fallen from a high peak to below 100,000 a year. At least there is room for those who are truly interested in the Brontës to enjoy the many exhibits. And the parsonage, like the landscape, is not being loved to death.

The Japanese, who read Emily Brontë's novel *Wuthering Heights* at school, have an affinity with its passion and tragedy which – comments Jane Sellars, director of the parsonage museum – mirrors their own literature. Almost half a million Japanese people a year visit Britain as tourists. 'When they come to Haworth they feel they are walking into the novel,' says Ms Sellars, while Tomimiko Ishikawa, leader of yet another party of Japanese tourists, finds the English scenery 'very calm' – and just loves the heather!

Haworth folk, needing a break from touristy matters, travel a few miles across the moor to have a quiet time at Heptonstall. Meanwhile, the daftest ideas about the talented sisters are certain to be taken up by the media and if anyone shoots a film within ten miles of Haworth, they dub the Brontë wind on to the sound track. Oh – that Brontë wind! It moans incessantly.

No one seems concerned with the Brontës' religiousness – with the fact that this was a Christian family. The moderns look for hidden meanings behind mundane events. The feminists have a field day. Television companies rake up personalities – who may or may not know where Haworth is – to introduce Brontë films. Scholars quote endlessly and boringly from Charlotte's letters to Ellen Hussey. The Japanese tourists appear to emulate the Brontës and record everything.

Virginia Stevens (later Virginia Woolf) took a fresh, lively approach to Brontë lore when she visited Haworth in 1904. Her account was the first of her prose writings to be published, heralding a sparkling career as an authoress. That first trip to Haworth was undertaken from Giggleswick, where she was staying with her cousin (headmaster of Giggleswick School) and his wife. The article appeared in the *Guardian*, a London weekly newspaper appealing mainly to clerics.

Virginia lingered before a case containing 'the little personal relics', which were Charlotte's dresses and shoes. 'The natural fate of such things is to die before the body that wore them,' she wrote, 'and because these, trifling and transient though they are, have survived, Charlotte Brontë the woman comes to life, and one forgets the chiefly memorable fact that she was a great writer. Her shoes and her thin muslin dress have outlived her.' Virginia toured Yorkshire's most memorable graveyard, where 'the stones seem to stare out of the ground at you in tall, upright lines, like an army of silent soldiers. There is no hand's breadth untenanted …'

The normally gentle Arthur Mee, in his classic series of guide books under the title *The King's England*, which he researched between 1936 and 1952, did not enthuse about Haworth, describing it as 'an unlovely place to which all pilgrims come ... we may think some sordid streak of fate made this grim place ... it is a depressing scene, set in the vast and terrible solitude of the moors.' Someone should provide these words with an organ accompaniment. Unlovely? Grim and depressing? Not today. Haworth is decked with the rainbow hues of tourism.

Harold Mitchell, the first full-time custodian of the parsonage museum, told me of the two old ladies who, having been shown round the building, which is decked with Brontëana, bade him goodbye. Then one of the ladies said: '*Who* did you say lived here?' I also heard from Harold about an American who stopped his car in Bingley and approached a pedestrian. 'Say – where did the Brontës live?'

The man who had been asked thought for a while, then replied: 'I can't help you. I'm a stranger in these parts. I come from Haworth ...'

Leeds is an exception in the Yorkshire context. It is vast, with many buildings scraping the sky. The Black Prince in City Square is not only black from city muck but also bemused at the swirling traffic. Leeds has its posh suburbs, its university, its huge redbrick Temple Newsam, and the multifarious activities which have created the business capital of the North. It also has its down-town areas, streets built on the classic gridiron pattern, with houses full of folk who have the full range of Yorkshire characteristics.

I think of a dear old lady who thought Kirkstall Abbey was a heavenly place, then added: 'It's a gurt pity they put it next to t'main road.' And the two road-sweepers, one of whom was speaking derisorily about his pal and said: 'Tha's all reight when tha's brushin' muck straight down gutter into t'grate but thar't licked when there's a bit of scientific work like going round a lampost.' An old lady, taken to her first orchestral concert at Leeds Town Hall, thought it was wonderful, saying: 'Ah just closed mi eyes – and I might have been listening to a radio.'

The populous mill-towns of the Southern Pennines are cleaner and tidier now that they have had the black skin of industrial muck scrubbed from them. James Gregson used to talk compellingly about the old mill-town days. He had some pithy speyks, or sayings, such as 'he's as uneasy as a dog wi' too monny fleas' and (of a woman who was not pleased) 'she's a face as black as t'fireback.'

These towns have had lots of characters. Ken Lemmon, a journalist who was proud of his West Riding background, told me of a spinster who, having listened to the Salvation Army band outside Morley Town Hall, beamed when the bandmaster came round with his hat and she placed a pound note in it. The delighted bandmaster said: 'Hallelujah. That's reight good on yer, missus. Yer can choose onny hymn yer want. What'll it be?'

The spinster replied: 'I'll have 'im what plays t'big drum.'

When a series of revival meetings took place, one of two brothers, who had a coil .[coal] business attended and was converted. Like the poacher turned gamekeeper, he now set about trying to convert his brother. Eventually, the brother 'telled him straight', observing: 'It's all varra well for thee to talk about being converted. And I can see it's med a difference. Tha's now a happy, good-living chap. But if I'm converted, who does ta think's going to weigh t'coil?'

Robert de Hode (Robin Hood) was not only a Wakefield lad; he was also a juvenile delinquent, having stolen some firewood. Later, he robbed in style, picking on prelates and merchants travelling on the forerunner of the Great North Road through the Forest of Barnsdale. The longbow of Little John, Robin's first lieutenant, is on view at Cannon Hall, near Barnsley. John himself was buried in the churchyard at the top of a steep hill in Hathersage, just over the Yorkshire–Derbyshire border. I asked two gossiping ladies the way to Little John's Grave. They directed me. Just before I left them, one said: 'Do you know what killed 'im?' I shook my head.

She remarked: 'That bloody hill!'

Which reminds me of some of the 'bloody hills': to be found in north-east of Yorkshire, where forty miles of heatherland terminate with splendid sea cliffs, much of the humour is concerned with roads which have such a tilt the driver of a car sees little more than the bonnet. Florence Hopper, of Driffield, stopped her car on a steep hill, in the Grosmont–Egton Bridge district, to ask an old lady if the hill was dangerous. The old lady said: 'No – not here. It's doon at t'bottom where they all kills thersens.'

Then there's the tale of a moorland farmer who drove straight out of a little hedge-bordered dale field into the path of a speeding car. The driver of the car stood on the brakes, then swerved into the field from which the tractor had come. The farmer turned to his son, sighed deeply, and said: 'By gum, lad, we nobbut just out of yon field in time.'

Garrowby Hill, long and steep, is the most famous stretch of road on the Wolds of south-east Yorkshire. The road from York begins a steady climb which leads to what is generally a quiet, little-known area where the countryside (though attractive) is not in the gee-whiz category beloved of the tourist industry. It was at a farm in a valley hardly anyone knows that I heard an amusing variation on the wedding wish – 'may all your troubles be little ones' – this being 'Congratulations. That's end o' thi troubles. Aye [pause] t'fore-end!'

Wit and humour bubble up wherever Yorkshire folk meet in a relaxed atmosphere. Such as the annual dinner of the Upper Wharfedale Agricultural Society, organisers of the celebrated Kilnsey Show. I was asked to be the chief speaker and told a few amusing tales, but the loudest applause was for the chairman, a man of few words. He remarked: 'Ah'm not going to say much. I'll just tell you a tale.'

He told of two old ladies who were sitting in the lounge of an owd-folk's home. One sighed and said: 'If I don't do something, I'll go daft. I think I'll strip off and 'streak' through t'lounge.' Which she did. Two short-sighted men were sitting near the door as she left the room. One said: 'Was that Edna?'

The other, with verbal austerity, said: 'Aye'.

The first remarked: 'Her dress wants ironing'.

And, of course, in a Yorkshire assembly, someone is bound to start singing 'Ilkla Moor Baht 'at', which is an early example of Yorkshire recycling with the faintest hint of cannibalism! I've heard 'Ilkla Moor' shouted by Rugby players, sung with delicacy at a party and rendered haltingly in the dining room of a hotel near the lavafields of Iceland by a company which was not entirely of Yorkshire origin.

The word baht is derived from the Anglo-Saxon 'butan', meaning 'without'. The lad who went courting had left his hat behind. That word baht has been the subject of much humour down the years. A dray which operated from stables at Saltaire had, written on the side, in yellow paint, 'Sir Titus Salt, Bart, Sons and Company Limited'. Gazing at it intently, a visitor remarked: 'Well, in spite of all, Sir Titus 'ed 'is ups an' darns i' life. He wor bart sons an' 'his company wor limited.'

The genesis of this song is said to have been in 1886 when a Halifax church choir had a summer picnic on the moor. During that picnic, a man and Mary Jane, the girl he loved left the party for a time. On their return, the choir party teased them, beginning with the famous words and being made up spontaneously. They sang to a hymn tune, 'Cranbrook', which had previously been used for *While Shepherds Watched*.

Everyone can start 'Ilkla Moor'. The test of true Yorkshireness is whether a person can finish it.

> Wheear wor ta bahn when Ah saw thee?
> On Ilkla Moor baht 'at.
>
> [The first line repeated twice; the second line thrice]
>
> Tha's been a-courtin' Mary Jane.
> On Ilkla Moor baht 'at.
>
> Tha's bahn ta get thi deeath o' cowd,
> On Ilkla Moor baht 'at.
>
> Then we sal ha ta bury thee.
> On Ilkla Moor baht 'at.
>
> Then t'worms'll come an' eit thee up.
> On Ilkla Moor baht 'at.
>
> Then t'ducks'll come an' eit up t'worms.
> On Ilkla Moor baht 'at.
>
> Then we sal come an' eit up t'ducks.
> On Ilkla Moor baht 'at.
>
> Then we sal hev etten thee.
> On Ilkla Moor baht 'at.

A team of Soviet folk singers, visiting England in the 1950s, heard the song from a Yorkshire coach driver when they were touring the provinces. They sang it from the stage of the Drury Lane Theatre in London, beginning:

Znai je my videli tebia
On Ilkla Moor baht 'at.

When pondering on Yorkshire humour, I decided to re-acquaint myself with a cross-section of Yorkshire and its people. I would walk for almost a hundred miles, from Keld (in the far west) to Robin Hood's Bay, overlooking the silvery sea. It was to prove a sure way of getting to know the people, their wit and humour. It did not confirm the Yorkshire reputation for taciturnity, which has been summed up as 'the ability to say nowt for a long time'. The descendants of the taciturn folk talk ten-to-the-dozen!

A Swaledale man reminded me of an H.L. Gee tale of a despairing servant girl who said to a friend: 'If I hadn't laughed mi 'ead off, I'd hev drowned missen!' And of the man whose wife had a prolonged stay in hospital and said, cheerfully: 'It was all on t'National Health. And remember, lad – while she wor in hospital, she was spending nowt!'

Slipping on a path, I scuffed my face and needed the services of a doctor to staunch the flow of blood. The medic was ensconced in a modern health centre. He had a modern way of treating small gashes. Instead of stitching it up, he stroked the wound (most carefully) with superglue, remarking: 'If you feel it stinging, don't move – or you'll have my finger stuck on your forehead for a few days.'

At Richmond, I heard two old men discussing a friend who was suffering from a serious complaint which was unspecified. One man remarked: 'Ah reckon only a post-mortem'd show what's wrang ... but he's that weak, he'd never stand it.'

My favourite medical tale is of the doctor who called at an updale farm and enquired about his patient, the farmer himself. Said the doctor to the farmer's wife: 'Does he take his medicine religiously?'

She replied: 'Nay, doctor – he curses every time I give him a dose.'

Wit is spontaneous. I complimented a Dales farmer on the view from his house. He replied: 'It won't pay t'rent.'

Another dalesman asked: 'How's ta doin'?' I replied, Yorkshire fashion: 'Not so good,' adding that the wolf was at the door.

He replied: 'It's aw reet as long as it doesn't whelp [drop its young] on t'mat.'

Old Mr Verity, a native of Nidderdale, told me of the Dales

farmer who married a second time, telling a friend: 'I thought it'd be nice to have someone to close mi eyes at t'end.' His friend retorted: 'Marriage oppened mine!'

Humour, which is contrived, often takes the form of a rambling tale. This goes down badly with busy people. In Yorkshire, the Nonconformist work ethic – 't'devil has work for idle hands' – is still evident among the older end. A West Riding farmer who had to listen to a wearisome tale from his wife became confused and, after ten minutes, said: 'Nay, lass – you'd better unravel it again.'

The rambling tale is permitted if the punchline is truly memorable, which it is in the case of the Yorkshireman who went to London and made his fortune frying fish and chips, beginning with a single shop and eventually owning a chain to rival Harry Ramsden's. One of his Yorkshire friends thought he'd like to go to London and do likewise, so he asked his now wealthy pal for the loan of some money to get him started. 'Nay,' said the tycoon, 'I came to an arrangement wi' t'Bank of England that if they didn't sell fish and chips, I wouldn't lend money.'

My stroll across Yorkshire led me through the Plain of York to the Vale of Mowbray, an area I had not visited for many years. The patchwork-quilt effect of fields with varying crops was enhanced by the startling yellow of oil-seed rape, grown as a source of oil. It was during a motor run in the Helmsley area that I saw my first field of rape. It looked from a distance as though a decorator had spilt a tin of yellow paint on the landscape. Seeing a middle-aged woman at a bus stop, I stopped to inquire the name of this new crop. She coloured up with embarrassment, and so did I, when she uttered the word 'rape'.

To a dalesman, the sight of a metallic monster, the combine harvester, rumbling across the big fields of the plain is a novelty. The 'combine' devours the crop and regurgitates it as a stream of grain, with the discarded straw being jettisoned to form a yellow ridge across the stubble. An arable farmer brought up wi' 'osses, binders and carts was fair-capped (astonished) at the sight of one of the newfangled combines. He remarked: 'Chap 'at invented that hed more' than nits in 'is 'eeard [head].'

Anyone who has bought such a monstrous piece of equipment is short of cash for a while. A Ripon newly-wed never seemed to have any money to flaunt. He told a friend he had become sick to death at his wife's nagging. She never stopped talking about money. 'Aye,' he said despairingly, 'ivvery time she sees me she

nags abaht brass. It happens morn, nooin an' neet.' His friend
asked what she did with all the money. The reply was: 'Nay – Ah
can't tell thee that. Ah haven't given her any yet.'

On my cross-Yorkshire walk I spent the last evening, before
taking to the Moors, at a pub where mine host whipped up trade
by making ordinary fare sound interesting. Instead of listing Game
Pie, he proclaimed: 'Hare, pheasant, venison, lead shot and
beater's finger.' In place of Sardines, he offered 'Two fat sardines'.
The demand for these two dishes had improved.

In Great Fryupdale, one of the glorious tributary dales of the
Esk, I overheard a woman talking about her husband who did the
shopping. He did not like doing it and complained both at home
and at the shop. His wife remarked: 'When he goes into a
supermarket, t'manager appears waving a white flag.' Another
woman had a husband who spent about an hour a day at home and
the rest of the time was down at the pub. The lady living next door
said: 'I'm so sorry.'

The wife remarked: 'Nay, lass – that hour soon passes.'

My walk across Yorkshire ended at the seaside. The blue
horizon appeared to view beyond a scraggy cliff-top patched with
the yellow of gorse blossom. A patrolling fulmar stared at me with
its cold arctic eyes. Herring gulls called titteringly, as though
responding to a doubtful story. I did not visit Whitby this time, but
I saw from afar the remains of the abbey with the blue sea beyond.
A small boy (it's always a small boy) who was taken to the abbey
asked his mother who had built it. Mother replied: 'The monks.'

He observed: 'Haven't they left it untidy?'

I was reminded of holidays spent in Whitby – and of the tale of
an old chap who, when he was about to have his first holiday at this
resort, was provided with new pyjamas. His daughter, who had
bought them, said: 'Be sure to wear 'em at night.'

He replied: 'Nay, lass – I nivver go anywhere at night – nobbut
bed!' So I reached the coast, turning south to Robin Hood's Bay.
An old Quaker friend thought it was a waste of time visiting the
sea. He said: 'It's only a horizontal line.'

Yorkshire, battered by bureaucracy, tormented by tourism and
television, is now largely a state of mind. The reality of a proud
county with three meaningful Ridings and a quirky boundary has
gone. The last great flowering of Yorkshireness was in the fifties
and sixties. Now, with so much altered and so many off-comers to
absorb, we have recourse to the in-jokes and concepts. In ten

years' time, Yorkshire will have a European outlook. Today's babies will live in the global village. This is why I have set down these recollections and amusing tales about the old Yorkshire and its people. Something of the Yorkshire spirit must endure.

2　Yorkshire Folk

Here's to me – and ma wife's husband –
Not forgettin' missen

The old-time music-hall comedians gave the impression that every Yorkshireman had a cloth cap on his head and a tyke (a small dog) at heel; he talked with clipped vowels, had a partiality for fish and chips, drank his tea out of a saucer (after wafting it with his cap) and said 'upsy-daisy' instead of 'excuse me'.

There's no such sub-species of the human race as *Homo sapiens Yorkshirii*. Travel through Yorkshire and you will meet the long and short and the tall. *Sapiens* means wise, which is not always the case with the Yorkshireman (the women are altogether smarter!). He can be stubborn on occasion. A famous old monologue relates how the Battle of Waterloo was held up when Sam Small's musket was knocked from his hand by a passing sergeant. And, as Sam said: 'Thou knocked it down, so thou pick it up.'

He persisted even when confronted by a succession of officers, each one mightier than the last. Sam did not retreat from the stand he had taken though armies were waiting to do battle, Napoleon was scheming and Blucher's men were not many miles away. Eventually, the Duke of Wellington himself pleaded with Sam, who relented, whereupon t'Iron Duke said: 'Let battle commence.'

The music-hall Yorkshireman was a West Riding man who liked to lie in bed in the morning and end the day with a pint of ale – a simple, satisfying life. Its success depended on a tolerant wife. Eric Knight, while in Canada, over five thousand miles away from his native Yorkshire, wrote entertaining tales about another Sam

Small – a bluff man who, by faith alone, learned to fly like a bird and change into a dog. Sam's 'better half' was known as Mully, short for Millicent, and when Sam impulsively said he loved her – a thing he had not said for nigh on twenty year – Mully sniffed and remarked: 'Ah took thee for better or worse, and happen it were worse than Ah thowt it would be.'

Knight gave us some choice Yorkshirisms, after asserting that 'as everyone knows, inch for inch and pound for pound a Yorkshireman's worth two from any other county – especially Lancashire'. He claimed for Yorkshire the prototype of a game which developed into golf. I refer to knurr and spell, which has a bat (of sorts), a small oblong piece of wood (the spell or billet) as a ball and demands quick reflexes, the 'spell' being tipped into the air, then hit as hard and as far as possible. 'Many years ago, this game drifted from Yorkshire up into Scotland where, in a much deteriorated and simplified form, it became known as golf.'

When trying to identify Yorkshire folk, the colour of the hair is no real guide. A dark-haired Yorkshireman is not necessarily descended from Celtic stock, nor a fair-haired woman from those Vikings who sailed their longboats up the Humber and Ouse to reach the heart of the county. A touch of ginger in the hair could represent an infusion of Irish, either as the result of a Norseman marrying an Irish lass before deciding to settle in northern England a thousand years ago or through Irish immigration at the time of the famine. It's a bit of a mix-up.

Talking of famine, there have been times when a Yorkshire family has been down to its last piece of bread and dripping. In more affluent times, the diet can be summed up in one word – stodge. You have to eat plenty to keep t'cold oot. A farm labourer who visited his local pub said he was 'that ravenous' he could 'eat a cawf [calf]'. The others disputed this. When he insisted, it was arranged he should return to the pub several days later and eat a calf. When he had left, there was a discussion as to how a calf might be presented and it was decided to do this in the form of three big pies. The farm labourer arrived, sat down and polished off the first pie. The second was pushed towards him. He ate that. When the third pie was produced, he protested: 'Nay – I'd better not touch that pie. I've got a cawf to eat toneet.'

Yorkshire parkin sticks to your ribs and plot toffee, which sticks to your dentures, is also known as Guy Fawkes toffee, after the Yorkshireman who tried to record a vote of no confidence in the government with a few tubs of gunpowder stacked in the cellar of the House of Commons. Bacon-and-egg pie replaces lost calories. So does Halifax pressed salt beef – three-and-a-half-pounds weight of beef, with some boiling bacon, carrots and onions, leeks, plus a pinch of this and a pinch of that to give it extra flavour. Wakefield pudding is cheap to make, for you stuff the middle with stewed apples you've cadged from your neighbour.

For Sunday tea, or a special occasion, you will need a stand pie, stuffed with beef or pork. A pie fresh from the shop is awash with warm gravy. Luvly! And, of course, there's the real native stuff – tripe and onions, with the tripe cut into bite-size pieces. Sheffield fish scallops involve four fillets of cod and four slices of potato of the same thickness as the fish. Yorkshire teacakes made a good snack. Yorkshire cheesecake is nothing like the clarty stuff now called cheesecake, a calorific experience.

Four million Yorkshire people, of all shapes and sizes, account for mini-mountains of parkin, plot toffee, tripe and scallops each week. Tastes as well as interests vary. All are bound together by pride in belonging to the county of broad acres. Every Yorkshireman is a patriot, and might remark – if he cared to waste time and energy on words – 'If tha's seen Yorksher, tha's seen England!' Women are rather less demonstrative. They let the men do the shouting. Socially, there's a wide range of people, from titled folk, with their big estates, who'd rather be seen dead than queuing for fish and chips, to the urchins of the mill-towns who don't mind queuing and, if the shopkeeper is not looking, will have a quick swig from the vinegar bottle.

Yorkshire folk get their priorities right. The well-being of Yorkshire comes first. Royalty has been entertained in the county of broad acres. It's a source of pride, but we don't get in a lather about it. A daughter of Queen Victoria married a Yorkshire earl and, according to old Johnny of Coverdale, who had a vivid imagination, and may just have been making it up, the owd Queen herself visited Wensleydale. When Johnny met her at Leyburn railway station, she said: 'Reach down that lile poke [bag] from t'rack, Johnny. It's a present for thee. We've been killing pigs at Windsor and I've brought thee some chitterlings [intestines].'

Queen Mary, wife of George V, haunted the antique shops of Harrogate and then asked her chauffeur to drive her to the top of Black Park, between Barden and Skipton, for some proper fresh air and a really good view. The King, who was recalled by one chap as 'a gingerish little fellow', was not seen indulging in the annual moor-rage called grouse-shooting but might be observed, on the following day, walking from Bolton Hall, home of the Duke of Devonshire, to attend worship in the priory church at Bolton.

Bolton Abbey is summat special in Yorkshire. (It was a priory, not an abbey, but the railway company changed the name to make it sound more appealing to potential travellers). In the big, preserved nave of Bolton a small girl completed her prayers with the request to 'make me a good little girl.' She whispered to her mother: 'I say that every day but it doesn't seem to make any difference.' The radio announcer's son who was taken to the Abbey included it at the tail-end of his evening prayers, when he said: And here, Lord, are the headlines again!'

Now and again, Yorkshire folk go to London and, reaching Westminster Abbey, ask where t'famous Yorkshire folk are buried. Or they may go to Wembley to collect a silver cup. If you hear someone making a fuss, it's just a Yorkshireman letting everybody know where he comes from.

The West Riding types (who featured in the old-time music-halls) love to drop aitches when there are posh folk about. They will wait for a while, then drop that aitch in such a way it has the impact of a dustbin lid hitting a concrete floor. Some railway passengers wiled away the time in guessing where each of them came from. 'You come from Lancashire,' said a Surrey man, referring to a lile chap in one corner.

'Nay,' he replied, 'I'm a Yorkshireman really. I haven't been feeling well lately.'

Back in Yorkshire, off-comers are quietly cut down to size. A London preacher at Langtoft Church made the mistake of asking some of his congregation afterwards how he had got on. A churchwarden said: 'Thoo didn't do too badly. Ah've 'eard worse!' Conversely, a Yorkshire bishop, who was a great scholar, on visiting a Dales parish church, was approached by the vicar and reminded that he was about to address 'a simple country congregation'. The bishop took the point and said he would adapt his sermon accordingly. He went too far. Afterwards, the vicar inquired of an old farmer what he thought of the preacher and was told: 'He was aw reet – but was he ever eddicated?'

Dr R.W.S. Bishop, a medical man on the North York Moors about the time of the 1914–18 war, was going too far when he compared one branch of the Yorkshire family with another. He concluded that Pennine folk 'are incomparably more witty than those of the Wolds or the Cleveland Hills'. Someone should enquire into the nature of his death.

Harry J. Scott, founder of *The Dalesman* magazine, pondered hard and long on the subject of dalesfolk, both those on the Pennines and others living in the quiet valleys of the North York Moors. Just before Harry and his wife retired from Clapham, in the shadow of Ingleborough, to Grange-over-Sands, on the sunset coast of Lancashire, he gave me a piece of well-thumbed card on which were pencilled as lecture notes his list of the main characteristics of the folk in rural Yorkshire. These were: realism, taciturnity, honesty, generosity and thrift.

Realism is derived from the dalesfolks' response to thin soils, to bad weather and to long, long winters. They live in an area where blue sky is usually about the size of a pair of Dutchman's breeches – to quote an old hay-time saying – and where everyone is thankful that the human skin is waterproof. A realist wrote with his finger on a filthy Land Rover parked at Hawes the words: 'Don't wash me – Plant summat.' You couldn't set that to music.

The realistic dalesfolk are great weather-watchers. A farmer was presented with a barometer to mark his silver wedding. A week or two later, the donor asked him how he liked it. 'Nay, Ah think nowt to it. It can't make up its mind. One day it says one thing and t'next day it says summat else.' Realism was a quality shared by a couple living in Upper Wharfedale who rang up relatives at Settle and mentioned a close friend who was ill. We'll call him Fred. They had been looking through their wardrobe but had nothing appropriate to wear if there was to be a funeral and so they intended to visit Moore's shop at Settle to buy some more clothes. They would call on the local relatives during that visit. They did not call. Months later, during another telephone conversation, the lady remarked: 'We didn't come to Settle after all. Fred got better.'

Taciturnity – a state of being sparing with words – is derived from the old-time isolation, when you soon 'talked up'. For centuries, until the turmoil of the First World War, dalesfolk lived their quiet lives and rarely went further than the local market town. The Dales farmer, out shepherding or gap-walling, almost lost the knack of talking. A regular infusion of news did come with the weekly newspaper. The postman could be relied on to give a round-up of local gossip. Mrs Brown, who lived at remote Cosh – a mile and a half from the head of Littondale, a tributary valley of the Wharfe – invited ramblers into her kitchen for cups of tea, so keen was she to learn about affairs in the outer world. No other habitation could be seen from her home.

I like the story of the First World War recruiting officer who arrived in a small Dales village which had heard about the war a week after it had been declared. The officer made directly for a man who was delivering milk, from kit to domestic can. 'My good man,' said the officer, briskly. 'Would you like to serve your King?'

The milkman replied: 'Aye – but I can nobbut spare a pint this morning.'

Yorkshire folk tend to be thrifty with words. A chemist was asked by a small boy for 'sixpennorth of ipecacuanha, please'. He then asked for it to be put down on Mum's account. The chemist, sighing deeply, requested his name. 'It's Thistlethwaite.'

Said the chemist: 'Take this stuff for nothing. I'm not going to spell ipecacuanha and Thistlethwaite for sixpence.'

One word suffices if you simply desire to hold your own in any Dales conversation, and that word is 'Aye'. Used sparingly, with differing inflections of the voice, it ensures continuity, even when the user does not understand what is being said because of the dialect or the complexity of the subject. Many years ago, while travelling by bus between Clapham and Skipton, I listened shamelessly to the conversation of two farmers sitting just across the aisle. One uttered a few words now and again. His friend parried with 'Aye'. On counting the ayes, I had reached ninety-nine by the time the bus stopped at the head of Skipton High Street, and I had collected yet another memorable quotation. A woman, addressing a fellow passenger, said: 'Alice nivver speaks to anybody. And when she does speak, she says nowt.' It's the sort of comment which Alan Bennett puts in his little notebook and uses in his Yorkshire plays.

Arthur Percival, a Yorkshireman who played with the Halle Orchestra, and who was a welcome visitor to *The Dalesman* office many moons ago, had a fund of tales, one of which illustrates the native ability to make a point in just a few words. The *Messiah* was being presented at a chapel where space was limited. The trumpeter's great moment would come in the famous aria, 'The Trumpet Shall Sound'. At rehearsal, he raised the long ceremonial trumpet to his lips and suddenly became aware that when it was extended to the playing position the bell of his instrument was only an inch or so from the ear of the principal cellist, who in the fortissimo climax would have to bear an awesome blast at zero range. The trumpeter leaned forward, tapped the endangered player on the shoulder and said, quietly: 'If Ah wer thee – Ah'd shift!'

In some circumstances, it is wise to be sparing with words. A man who sold a horse said to the purchaser: 'It doesn't look so good.' The purchaser declared: 'It looks aw reet to me.' He brought it back a few hours later, complaining that the horse was blind in one eye. The seller reminded him that he said it didn't look so good. Perhaps it's another version of the man in a horse story which appeared in my father-in-law's farming repertoire. This man, having sold a horse to a friend, returned the animal with the remark: 'It wean't 'od its head up.'

Said the farmer: 'Yon's a proud hoss. It's ashamed. Thee get it paid for!'

Harry Scott illustrated his point about honesty by saying that if a parcel was inadvertently left in Settle on market-day, which is Tuesday, it would still be there in the following week. We might return to t'chapel for evidence of honesty in speech. W.H. Blakeston, of Driffield, said that Wolds preachers were much too wise to expect praise, even if they excelled themselves. He had preached his best at a small chapel. Afterwards, the steward remarked: 'At least we've had a good sing.' It was a different matter when Dr W.E. Sangster, one of Methodism's great preachers, was a minister at Leeds. After a particularly stirring sermon, a member of the congregation said: 'By gum, lad – thou'd have made a champion Yorkshireman.'

Generosity was widespread in the days before the car offered a person high mobility. It usually took the form of an invitation to 'have a cup o' tea', which turned out to be a full meal, with apologies that 'there's nowt warm'. Tommy Marshall, of Greenhow Hill, was a Methodist preacher who walked many a mile to appointments. At one remote chapel, after the morning service, no one invited him to dinner. Never lost for words, young Tommy went up to the most prosperous farmer he could see and said: 'Would you like to come home with me for dinner?'

The farmer said: 'How far does ta live?'

'About six miles.'

The farmer pondered for a while, then smiled and said: 'Nay, lad – thou'd better come home wi' us.'

Many are the tales told of Yorkshire thrift. A Yorkshire farmer, meeting a woebegone friend at the market, heard of financial problems and offered to call round and advise him on how to be thrifty. The two men met round a fire. The visitor said: 'Just wait a minute while I put out that paraffin lamp. We don't need t'light on when we're nobbut talking ...' Nothing was thrown away. 'It might come in.'

If anything was lost, then it had to be found. Lettice Cooper, a Yorkshire-born novelist, told of a Leeds businessman who, on a visit to a London hotel, could not find his hat. The silver-tongued manager eloquently defended the honour of his hotel. He offered abject apologies. He could not understand what had happened. It had never happened before, etc. When a gap occurred in the flow of silvern words, the hat's owner, distrustful of fancy words and getting right back to basics, declared: 'Where's my blooming hat?'

Old concepts and loyalties live on in the hearts of t'older end. Old-time dancers still swirl and sing to the strains of 'My Girl's a Yorkshire Girl'. J.B. Priestley, who loved the Dales, wrote of the dalesfolk as being like 'minor characters from Ibsen' and of a glutton who was 'digging his grave with his knife and fork'. When Priestley died, he was cremated and the ashes eventually came to rest in the yard of Hubberholme Church at the head of Wharfedale. For several weeks before the funeral service took place, Priestley (in ash form, reposing in an urn) lay under the stairs at a local farm. The situation would have appealed to his Yorkshire sense of humour.

Priestley, a thoroughbred Yorkshireman, did not miss a chance of trumpet-blowing. When, in what is doubtless an apocryphal tale, an admirer said to him: 'I think your *Angel Pavement* is the most wonderful book ever written', the author is said to have replied: 'And what's wrong with *The Good Companions*?'

Today, in Bradford, Priestley's native city, an ever-varying, distorted impression of the Victorian town appears in reflection on the windows of a modernistic police headquarters just across the road, providing images which budding David Hockneys might contemplate. The city centre crowds include a host of women wearing colourful saris – ten per cent of the city's population is Asian.

The original Asian settlers were brought in to augment the labour force at the local mills. Priestley would have readily absorbed them in his literary work. Already, there's a Yorkshireness about their speech and also their determination to make good. Yorkshire drive is illustrated by the man whose job at a West Riding hotel was to clean boots. He was teased about this by someone who thought he would surely become the proprietor. He replied: 'There's no chance. Chap 'at owns the place also comes from Yorksher.'

H.L. Gee, a Yorkshire Methodist with a lively pen, looked for the elusive Yorkshireman and concluded:

> Diversity of character makes each of us distinctive, but this common trait is our peculiar failing. The most uncouth and blatant Yorkshireman breathing, complete with heavy jowl and rude stare, is probably nothing more than a mass of inferiority complexes ... Often we make a show of being unnecessarily forthright because we are anything but sure of ourselves.

He may have been right. We do like to 'pull folk to pieces' or 'cut folk down to size', especially the parson. It's done dryly. After a particularly long sermon, a parishioner said: 'T'owd vicar finished ages ago – bud he wouldn't stop.'

Gee mentioned the reticence of many Yorkshire lads to express their love for the opposite sex. Willie Cockrem, a West Riding lad, was so shy his mother was delighted one evening when he brushed his hair and announced: 'Ah'm bahn down t'village to see yon lass o' Dysons.' On his return, she asked if he had seen her. 'Aye,' replied Willie proudly. 'And if Ah 'adn't bobbed dahn behind t'hedge, she'd hev seen me.' Eventually, Willie and the lass o' Dysons started 'walking out'. They stood watching two cows rubbing their faces together. Said Willie, feeling very bold: 'Ah can do that.'

His girlfriend replied: 'Well, I can't stop thee. It's not my cow.'

In marked contrast was the Yorkshireman who was 'wed' four times. One day, as he returned home after burying his fourth wife, he met the squire, who – winking at him – said: 'You've always managed to marry women with money.'

The old Yorkshireman replied: 'Aye, but what wi' t'funeral expenses, there isn't much profit.' He didn't object to being hen-pecked and told the squire: 'It's not bad – being pecked wi' t'reet hen!'

A clergyman who visited a house where husband and wife were having a noisy argument pointed to the dog and cat sleeping by the hearth. The vicar commented on how peaceful they were. 'Aye,' said the husband, 'but thee tie 'em together – an' see what 'appens.'

One of the most delightful H.L. Gee stories concerns Helmsley, an area presided over by Lord Feversham. A local man who claimed to know everyone of importance overheard a conversation about his lordship in a local public house. The braggart remarked: 'Oh, aye, Ah knaws 'im.'

One of the group said, quietly: 'Mebbe thoo diz and mebbe thoo dizzn't. What I'd like to knaw is – diz Lord Feversham knaw thee?'

Yorkshire types include the lean, lithe, taciturn men of the High Pennines (in so-called Herriot Country), the mill-town folk and those from the industrialised areas of the North East. Some urban types are descended from dalesfolk who moved following the collapse of lead-mining, a once great industry. When I gave a talk on the Dales at Colne, the audience was almost entirely made up of such folk, each inordinately proud of his or her Yorkshire origins. The Yorkshireman who stays at home is quick to assert his Yorkshire background. One, an aged gardener, quickly added 'ah've bin in this garden for fifty year and I still puts in a good day's work. That's not bad for an octogeranium.'

I've always been impressed by the distinctive communities along the Yorkshire coast where the old fishing villages cling to the cliffs like martins' nests. The coast-dwellers once formed a quite distinctive community, cut off from the world by moorland. Those who live at villages on the plain have viewpoints of what is basically one third land, two-thirds sky. Nowadays, much land is set-aside, as part of a scheme organised by the EEC. In the old days, every yard mattered. Scarecrows were made to keep birds off the grain crops. One scarecrow looked so alarming, the farmer claimed he'd seen pigeons returning with some of the corn they'd taken.

In Yorkshire, as I shall continually remind you, cricket was elevated to the status of a religion, with men such as Hutton, Boycott and Trueman as its high priests. Among an earlier generation of Yorkshire greats was Herbert Sutcliffe. He agreed to take part in a charity match between two village teams. A huge crowd waited for the action. He was stumped first ball. 'Owzat!' yelled the triumphant wicket-keeper. The umpire gave him a withering glance and said: 'Not aht.' In a quieter voice, intended only for the wicket-keeper, he said: 'Folk haven't come here to watch thee stump.'

For every test match which takes place at Headingley, there are scores of local matches in which rivalry is just as keen. Cricket is played on pitches situated in a green hollow among the Moors. Harry Mead tells the story of playing in an away match when in the first four balls, 'their' umpire disallowed two l.b.w. appeals by the visitors' opening fast bowler, who was also the captain. Hitching his trousers for the task ahead, he bellowed: 'Right, lads, we'll get nowt here. We'll just have to bowl this lot out.'

A man who arrived at a country railway station with plenty of time to catch his train watched an impromptu cricket match, with the station-master batting while balls were delivered by his porter. The station-master slogged the balls all over the area. The visitor asked if he could have a go at bowling, and he got the batter out first ball. Said the relief porter: 'Thank goodness for that. He's bin in for five months.'

Rugby is a highly competitive sport. When the ball had been kicked right out of the ground and a further upsurge of violence seemed likely, a voice from the stand was heard to say: 'Don't bother wi' t'ball, lads. Get on wi' t'game.'

Alien influences are at work on our Yorkshire culture. Television is blurring the old images. The James Herriot tales, re-told by the BBC as *All Creatures Great and Small*, came from a master story-teller who was reared in Glasgow but during his stay in the Dales evoked most authentically the character and speech of dalesfolk. It was a pity that a host of off-comers were enrolled to play the leading roles in the BBC series, which lost the 'rough edge' of Northern life, especially when the authentic Herriot tales ran out and London-based script writers provided additional material.

As a writer, Alf Wight (to use his proper name) had a light touch. When I met him, after he had had a physically stressful time, I thought he looked contented and relaxed. His face was 'a good colour', as we say in Yorkshire, partly because he had been out and about in the garden or on the hills during a sunny spell. When I mentioned 'colour', he laughed and recalled his young days as a vet visiting the dalehead farms with their memorable residents. 'When they said you had a bad colour, you got worried. I'm not a very ruddy individual really, but they would say: "Thou's lost a bit o' ground since I saw you last, Mr Wight." Or: "I think you've failed a bit, you know." '

In the early 1940s, the vet had little to help him and he came across farmers who were using some methods not far removed from black magic.

That was probably what motivated me to write a book in the first place. It was a very funny time in veterinary practice. All those awful old treatments. A cow went down. The farmer would say it had a worm in its tail. The cow couldn't get up so they cut its tail off. Another farmer kept a billy goat (which stank) in the shippon to prevent contagious abortion. He thought the smell would help cure the complaint. Yet abortion hit a herd only once. Then the animals developed an immunity. The herd was all right next year. The billy goat got the credit.

Alf Wight had driven to the dalehead farms and met a kind-hearted people. He remembered chatting with a man, aged about sixty. 'Just over the fell-top, some five miles away as the crow flies, was some marvellous countryside. He had never been there. He lived in his own little dale and went to Leyburn on market-day. And that was that ...'

The North York Moors around Goathland have become *Heartbeat* country. The title *Heartbeat* was given to a TV series based on the work of Nicholas Rhea, a Yorkshire writer. Yorkshire Television brought in an actor from *Eastenders* to give it extra appeal, which it did, claiming the attention of nearly eighteen million viewers. At once-peaceful Goathland, which lies in a green saucer ringed by purple moorland, and where an old Swaledale sheep used to drop her lamb in the shadow of the churchyard wall, the fans arrive looking for the fictional Aidensfield.

During the spring bank-holiday, 1995, the *Heartbeat* appeal attracted 15,000 people, who had travelled in 5,000 cars. Add to this the luxury buses which have evolved until they are like shiny hotels on wheels. There must have been a half-mile queue at the toilets. It has been suggested that the National Park authority should build a coach park out of the village, enlarge the village park and make a decent footpath from one end of Goathland to another. A local landowner (descendant of the poet William Wordsworth, who sparked off the Lakeland tourist trade) has devised a Goathland exhibition centre, including *Heartbeat* memorabilia, such as the original Triumph Herald car used in the first series.

The *Heartbeat* series is sold abroad. What sort of an impression of Yorkshire life does it create in the hearts and minds of off-comers? The scriptwriters pack more action into one episode than the local bobby used to experience in his whole career. Into Goathland/Aidensfield, during the warmer months of the year, gaggles of tourists – camera-toting Japanese, gee-whizzing Americans and families from the low countries looking for moors and mountains – destroy the old-time character of the village. An Australian family, travelling through wintry Britain in a camper van, made a special detour to see the setting for the television spectacular.

Down in what used to be known as t'West Riding are two television honeypots – Holmfirth and Esholt, associated with the BBC's *Last of the Summer Wine* and Yorkshire TV's *Emmerdale*, which used to be *Emmerdale Farm*, situated at Arncliffe, until that area became so popular with *Emmerdale* fans the actors and camera crew were tripping over them. *Emmerdale*, which has run to over two thousand instalments, is now raw soap, and as Yorksher as haggis. At least it provides income for the Esholt post office, the pub and local people who have allowed their property to be used in the filming (which carefully avoids including the feature for which Esholt has long been known – its high-tech sewage works).

Holmfirth, a somewhat rundown little industrial town, was reinvigorated by *Last of the Summer Wine*. The tourists flock in, responding to the lure of a television series which has come as close as any programme to catching that elusive Yorkshireness. And still they come! Yorkshire Television, who produced the first soap documentary (about Jimmy's, the nickname for a famous Leeds hospital) have also chronicled a season in the life of Primrose Valley, near Filey. It is a holiday park, not a camp. The BBC series entitled *Hi De Hi*! ensured that we will never again take the holiday camp idea seriously. (This valley doubtless boasted primroses in the early days, when a few caravans came to a halt in a local farmer's field).

A survey by an association of travel agents called ARTAC World Choice reflects Yorkshire's growing popularity with tourists – or what a friend calls touriods! The county already attracts seven million visitors a year, many of whom 'do' a village an hour, looking over the bridge at the river, and having a ploughman's lunch at the pub, where in some cases their feet slur on good Yorkshire stone and the décor of the bar is just as it was carried out in Victorian times.

A Dales pub I visited recently had a notice pinned on the front door: 'Please leave the Pennine Way outside.' The tourists, having had their gargantuan snacks, with enough food to put a ploughman to sleep for the afternoon, then dash off to see the church, with its smell of foisty hymn books, and leave their names, places of origin and comments in the visitor's book.

Real old Yorksher humour is pithy. A traveller, visiting a Dales farm, asked a bystander: 'Where's the master of the house?'

The labourer replied: 'She's in t'kitchen.'

When a man reported that his uncle was ninety-one years old and had just stopped riding his bike, a Yorkshire response was: 'What's up; has 'e had a puncture?' A young doctor from overseas who picked up most of his English while working in a Bradford hospital said to one patient: 'Nah, lad, oppen thi gob and let's have a lewk at thi lollicker.'

Finally, I relate a story of the 98-year-old who had the real Yorkshire spirit. After having his photograph taken by a breezy young press photographer, he was cordially thanked and the photographer hoped he would have the pleasure of taking the picture of the old chap when he became a centenarian. The veteran looked him up and down and said: 'Ah don't see why thou shouldn't. Tha looks pretty fit to me.'

3   In the Beginning

Ther's nowt so queer as fowk.
[One of the best known Yorkshire sayings.]

For centuries, Yorkshire folk had to 'scrat' for a living. An
archaeologist who took me to a site at what was once the edge of a
glacial lake, near Pickering, pointed excitedly to a thin charred
layer – evidence, he thought, of an early settlement. I prefer the
conventional caveman theory, as expounded by my old friend Tot
Lord, of Settle.

Tot took life at a leisurely pace. He let the rest of the family run
the Lords' greengrocery business while he lived the life of a
Victorian gentleman, devoting himself to archaeology, sport,
reading back numbers of *Country Life*, chatting with his cronies,
going back to nature – with a gun – and regularly visiting the Nuvic
Cinema, where he had his own seat.

His sporting activities were written about by E.H. Partridge,
head of Giggleswick School, who was also a devotee of field sports
when they were fashionable. He recalled seeing Tot Lord's red
face 'which in the fading light [of the Ribble Valley] had the dull
glow of old baked brick'. Tot brought down what he described as a
'white goose'. To an ornithologist it was a whooper swan, which
was far more than a mouthful. The remnants languished in Tot's
larder for weeks.

Wrote Partridge, of Master Tot the archaeologist: 'His actual
calling is a matter of no moment. It occupies the smallest part of
his time and his attention. His sidelines are legion and speculation
is the salt of his life … His passion is archaeology in which his
labours are prodigious and disinterested.' Indeed. He looked more

like a gamekeeper than a greengrocer. There was a 'dibber' at the end of his walking stick – a short blade which was ideal for demolishing mole-heaps in case some ancient flint instruments had been thrown up by the industrious mammals.

The sight of Tot in repose was a memory to cherish. He would be sitting on the verandah of Town Head, which was decked by wicker furniture and the skull of an elephant. His ragged garden, the lurking place of *Felis domesticus* had a splendid centrepiece in a palm tree. Tot's private museum, which was entered after a ceremony of the keys far more elaborate than that in the Tower of London, contained bones and artefacts found in local caves where (it was assumed) hyenas had denned in primeval times, dragging in the bones of their prey. Early Man would find shelter here from climatic excesses and creatures who regarded him as a prey item.

Tot was an authority on Yorkshire's Bone Age the oldest specimens, dug out from under a thick layer of glacial clay, and dated by Tot's scientific pals at about 120,000 years. Those prehistoric beasts (an early form of elephant, hippo and rhinoceros – not the scientists!) doubtless enjoyed the good years between two glaciations. It was fascinating to hear Tot speculating that we are living in an interglacial period and that rather than warming-up, our part of the earth will be suddenly and spectacularly chilled.

Much more recent in Tot's museum were the bones of Ice Age mammals like reindeer and the great cave bear, which appears to have been a cuddly, affable beast. It spent most of its life sleeping. Tot's collection included a bone found below the layer of glacial clay. No one could be sure whether it was man or beast. Tot called it the bone of contention. A Victorian excavator who worked in Victoria Cave lost a tooth and could not resist sticking it in the pre-glacial layer. Any normal excavator would have been buried alive but he was a Birkbeck, from Anley, and so there was a round of good-natured laughter.

Above the clay deposited when the area was the playground of glaciers were traces of (fanfare of trumpets) – Yorkshire caveman. Hurrah!

Tot had little to show of the male aspect of prehistory but he exhibited, in a sitting posture, the collection of bones found in a limestone pavement of the lady (if such there be at that remote time) who became known as Ingleborough Woman. She was no beauty, especially as displayed by Tot. Space in the museum was limited. He could allocate only half of one showcase to her. And I gathered from Tot that early folk were a poor-looking lot, with stooped posture and arthritic limbs not at all like the Flintstones of recent cartoon fame.

Ingleborough Woman was at least in good company. Neatly lined up in glass-topped cases, were big bones, little bones, half-gnawed bones, slivers of bones and calcined bones. A reverse-barbed harpoon, made of deer horn, evoked thoughts in Tot's mind of Early Man fishing in the glacial lakes. When I took J.B. Priestley to see the collection, someone remarked: 'To understand this lot, you would have to get into the mind of Early Man.' And Priestley, taking his pipe out of his mouth and speaking with a voice made nationally familiar through his wartime postscripts on the radio, declared: 'The main thing today is to get out of the mentality of Early Man.'

Both Sir Arthur Keith and Dr Arthur Raistrick loved Tot's quirkish personality and droll ways. It was Arthur who told me that when Tot was excavating at Cave Ha', to the north of Buckhaw Brow, he arranged for his wife (who was also a member of the vast Lord family) to deliver his Sunday dinner. And when Tot erected a tent on Malham Moor, he slept in a 'proper' bed with a headpiece made of brass.

The folk who inhabited the world of Tot's imaginings would be preoccupied by food-gathering. Joy was doubtless unrestrained when someone felled a red deer and there was a squabble for the three hundred pounds of juicy red flesh. By-products from that kill – bone, sinew, skin – were converted into useful objects, the cured skins as clothing or, with several sewn together, for the prototype of the tent.

The Iron Age folk, emotionally well developed, had craftsmen who made dragonesque brooches. Was Victoria Cave really a habitation – or, with its fine assembly of ornamental objects, a tribal mausoleum? I could never open Tot up on the subject. All the objects were given to Giggleswick School and exhibited for years in the old grammar school, which was demolished.

It is said that Tot, with his usual good luck, saw Tommy Moorby, with horse and flat cart, conveying material from the old school to the tip. Tot recognized in the rubble some of the old Victoria Cave material which, of course, he kept. And who can blame him when otherwise (if the story is true) it would have been buried for another few thousand years?

Apart from red deer, which would be the culinary jackpot, a Yorkshire Bone Age cook might serve up some baked hedgehog, a badger steak, grilled trout or stewed duck. (It is not known when Yorkshire Pudding was first sampled and a Victorian claim that it was first mixed by a visiting angel has not been taken seriously). Coastal dwellers laboriously knapped molluscs from the rocks or pounced on any fish left in pools by the ebb tide. (Yorkshire folk had to wait until the days of the first Queen Elizabeth, and the introduction of the potato, before they could marry fish to chips under the exuberant slogan: 'Frying Tonight'.)

The hunter-gatherers gradually evolved into farmers. They tackled the light, well-drained soils of the south-east Wolds and Limestone Craven. When the climate ameliorated the people spread on to the tacky peatlands of the High Pennines and doubtless began to use the word 'clarty', for the landscape stuck to their feet.

Trees blocked many a good view and limited the area which could be farmed. A slash-and-burn technique was messy. Neighbours tended to complain of the smoke. It was better to ring-bark the trees or save up for a Great Cumbrian Axe, made of volcanic tuff from central Lakeland, which you could buy at the nearest stone circle, when there was a tribal gathering.

When trees had been felled, the rocks remained. Stone-bashing and clearance of land went on for years. Hernias would be added to the prehistoric conditions – stooped frame and arthritis. What to do with the unwanted stone was a problem. It might be piled up to provide walls for a house. The wind whistling through the cracks would take away the BO and the cooking smells. Stones were also heaped up as walls to restrain the stock and deter the local wolves.

As they snuggled by the fire on winter neets, did early folk – these hard, undemonstrative, matter-of-fact pioneers in the Yorkshire wilderness – tell funny stories? Add a few guttural sounds to the ageless tales. Was there a chorus of groans when someone asked: 'What's that funny noise?'

'An owl.'

'I know that – but what was 'owling?'

By this time, self-respecting denizens of what was to become Yorkshire were putting the best stones aside to make barrows, not of the wheeled variety but burial places – stone chambers, covered with earth. From a distance they looked like great lumps o' muck until they were grassed over. In gentle country, long barrows were made. Up t'Dales, where folk have always done things differently, they fancied circular ones. The bones of the dear-departed were burnt/calcined before being stored away. It was space-saving. Pottery and bits of lint were left beside the remains, a form of insurance against hardship in any future existence.

As time went on, there were so many barrows, standing stones, recumbent stones, boundary stones, and stones which had been erected just for the fun of it, you could scarcely walk ten yards without barking your shin. At Boroughbridge, people came for miles to look at what would become known as the Devil's Arrows. The Devil must have had a hernia. Visiting tribesfolk gawped at an enormous monolith at Rudston, near Bridlington. They must have been a pious lot at Rudston, having a religious centre and gatherings which would be free of sermons or a collection. On Ilkley Moor, some ancient artist cut the swastika (a good luck sign) into the sandstone outcrops.

The Iron Age was a miserable time in West Yorkshire, which caught the full force of the Atlantic weather. It did nowt but rain. Early folk worshipped natural gods, such as the spirit of rivers and wells. No one worshipped rain. They just tolerated it and rejoiced that the human skin is waterproof. One group, with nothing better to do, carved stone heads.

The Celtic folk, who were known as Brigantes, were riled when the swaggering Romans arrived, with armour clanging and the sun glinting on the prototypes of riot shields. Having tidy minds, the Romans introduced bureaucracy. There was endless form-filling. You couldn't get a thing unless you had signed for it. They had their noses blooded by the Caledonians and therefore built a wall from Solway to Tyne. They didn't try to conquer the Brigantes, building a few forts, linking them with good roads and policing the area. Did you hear the story of the Roman centurion who lined up his men and said: 'From the left number.' They did: 'I, II, III, IV, V ...'

The Brigantean queen, Cartimandua, enthusiastically embraced Roman luxury and also embraced a Roman standard bearer. Her husband, Venutius, whipped up Brigantean fervour and had a showdown with the Romans at Stanwix, near what is now Barnard Castle. He was defeated. Cartimandua got her come-uppance (being boiled in oil) and the Romans outstayed their welcome by several hundred years.

When they cleared off, or shut up, their buildings fell into ruin, leading one early Yorkshire lad to ask, with all his northern charm: 'Who brok 'em?' We Yorkshire folk got back to squabbling among ourselves – till the Angles and Saxons and Danes arrived. They were a solemn lot, but good workers. They showed us how to clear t'countryside. The northern folk had their pagan gods, including Heck. He was invoked by the lusty cry of 'By Heck!' The Northumbrians were converted to Christianity by some gentle Celtic monks from Iona. A simple country lad called Caedmon astonished everybody by bursting into song. His hymn about the Creation led to him being called the father of English song.

Another lot of monks, led by Augustine, landed from the south, got the upper hand at a Synod at Whitby, in AD 664. Here a religious house had been founded by Hilda in AD 657. It endured until the Synod and the triumph of the po-faced monks from Rome, whose rule triumphed. The city of York was a centre of learning when much of England was still groping about in the Dark Ages. Monks from medieval York rekindled the light of Christianity in parts of Europe.

The Vikings arrived as rapists, arsonists and pillagers – or so they'd like you to think – and many stayed on as settlers. One group came in from the east and followed the big river up to York. Others, from stock which had colonised northern Scotland, with footholds in Ireland, infiltrated the dale country from the west with red-haired Irish wives and lots of children. These Irish-Norse picked the remaining (poor) land, around the daleheads.

A family would overwinter in a large farm situated in the dale and, in summer, the low land would be quit (to grow grass for hay) while the women and children made for the fells to tend stock which took advantage of the summer flush of grass. Their summer residences were called saeters. Now they are occupied the year through, as in the ABC of Wensleydale – Appersett, Burtersett and Countersett.

The only amusing tale to survive from these days is of the boy who had never spoken until, one day, his mother set the usual helping of Yorkshire pudding in front of him and he said: 'It's 'orrible.'

Overjoyed at hearing her son speak, the mother asked why he had not spoken before.

Said the lad: 'Yorkshire pudding's allus bin aw reight till now.'

Another batch of Norse folk went southwards, settled in northern France, became sophisticated (they talked posh and developed big ideas) and eventually invaded England as 'the Normans'. There were folk of Norse stock everywhere! The old Vikings [named after the viks, or creeks of their native Scandinavia] had taken York in AD 867 and divided Yorkshire into three parts, each of which was a 'thirding' or third, with the addition of a self-contained Ainsty of York. The main divisions became the West, North and East Ridings. Each Riding was sub-divided in to Wapentakes. (Now read it again, slowly, or you'll forget it.)

The blood which courses through the veins of Yorkshire folk therefore includes a bit of Celt, possibly a dab of Italian, via those hussies who hung around the troops at Eboracum (York) or Danum (Doncaster), some Anglian, Danish and Norse, with a minor infusion of Norman. And that's just for a start!

King Billy, more widely known as William the Conqueror, his lords and their retainers, gave us a rotten time. It's no wonder there's no love lost between us and the French. The Normans were not only arrogant; they could also be peevish. When we demonstrated our Yorkshire spirit by having a lively rebellion, they took umbrage to the extent of razing the settlements to the ground. There was so much pillaging, destroying and burning that when the Domesday scribes set to work (AD 1086) to make a record of who had what (for taxation purposes) a lot of the ground was marked, simply, as 'waste'.

Then these Normans divided up the land – our land – and put up their blasted castles everywhere. The ordinary folk, remembering the scorched earth policy of the touchy Normans, kept their heads down for a while and, untypically, said nowt they might regret. (Hence the Yorkshire expression already quoted: 'Hear all, see all, say nowt.')

The Norman lord, secure behind his castle walls, having the best of food, including fresh fish from his ponds and fresh venison from his park, took out an insurance policy to ensure he'd do well in the hereafter. He gave property and much else to the monks. They agreed to pray for his soul till the end of time (or until the reign of Henry VIII, whichever was the earliest). There were white monks (Cistercians, who developed an obsession over sheep) and black monks (including Augustinian canons, who moved from draughty Embsay to some prime land beside the upper Wharfe at Bolton). Yorkshire had nuns galore.

Monks were supposed to live frugal, prayerful lives. They lived very well, thank you, and contrived to show a profit, except when the Scots were being a nuisance, raiding down as far as Yorkshire, killing and pillaging. Now and again, when the Church authorities checked up on the monasteries and nunneries, they were displeased. Sex reared its ugly head, though not as often as lurid modern novels might have you believe. The Yorkshire climate is generally too cold and damp for orgies.

At Bolton Priory, by the Wharfe, life was a round of prayers and duties which must have become tedious to any who lacked a full measure of piety. The canons did eat well – mainly bread, pottage and ale, supplemented by meat, fish and dairy products. Food was available from the priory farms. Two-thirds of the cash expenditure for the kitchen went in the purchase of fish, with no mention of chips.

'Being familiar', as prudish Yorkshire mothers were to call it, was just one of a number of enjoyable sins. The nuns of Nun Appleton were sometimes to be found quaffing ale (if not cider) at the local inn. At Egglestone, where the brothers were quarrelsome, the prior was instructed to spend more time at home 'without gadding here and there'. When Archbishop Melton visited Bolton in 1321, he was supposed to enquire into the state of local life but found time for hunting, having brought with him – a pack of hounds!

The Cistercians were by and large an industrious lot. At Fountains Abbey, in the Valley of the Skell, near Ripon, they said prayers and counted sheep. It's no wonder they slept such a lot for they had maybe 50,000 sheep. At Jervaulx, the monks were renowned for their Wensleydale cheese (made from the milk of ewes – ugh!) and for the quality of their horses, which they reared in the limestone country of North Ribblesdale, where there are reminders of their enterprise in Studfold and Colt Park.

After the prosperous years came the long monastic decline. The monks, being inclined to put Mammon before God, often got their sums wrong. Fountains became deeply in debt to Italian merchants who had bought 'futures' in wool. It's the old familiar story of wanting to get rich quick. The abbot was spending money he hadn't got. Early in the fourteenth century, some monasteries were visited by pestilence (not the tax inspectors, but the Black Death). Henry VIII dissolved the monasteries. The benefactors of yesteryear who had planned for everlasting prayers must now have been sleeping uneasily in their tombs.

Then we Yorkshire folk got back to airing our differences. The Yorkshire tradition of rebellion was maintained during what was called the Pilgrimage of Grace, which was neither a pilgrimage nor graceful, especially as the leaders were hanged. There followed, in due season, the Wars of the Roses. This accounted for about thirty years of the fifteenth century. It wasn't a dispute between gardeners, but an unholy row between the Houses of York and Lancaster. Some Yorkshiremen supported the Lancastrian cause and vice versa, which made life confusing. Like rugby players plastered with mud, you could never be sure who was your enemy.

The conflagration was never properly dampened down. It flares up from time to time along the Yorkshire–Lancashire border and also in the sporting arenas of Headingley and Old Trafford, where (once again) there's confusion, all the players wearing white. In the seventeenth century, a civil war kept every Yorkshire nerve on edge. The bloodiest clash was on Marston Moor, which the Roundheads won 1-nil. Cromwell, a good Christian man, said: 'God made them as stubble to our swords.' There must have been quite a few Christians in the stubble. (And talking of stubble, a farmer at Bolton in Wharfedale got very annoyed when Prince Rupert, *en route* with his Royalist Army to Marston Moor, camped in his best cornfield overnight.)

When everyone was weary of fighting, they dispersed. Those who earlier had bought monastic land now set about developing it. They had confidence now that people had got fighting out of their system and they might confidently bequeath their land and property to their descendants without someone coming along and pinching it. So they demolished the old wooden houses, with their coverlet of thatch, opened up a few quarries, and built in stone and slate. It would take more than an easterly wind to lift that lot! The houses tended to look alike, with their porches, mullion windows and dripstones (for plastic guttering would not be invented for another three hundred years).

Yorkshire was beginning to look tidy again. Pride of belonging bubbled up in the hearts of its native folk. George Hicks, who was born near Northallerton, preached a sermon in London in 1682 and told the smug Southerners: 'Our county, as the curious observe, is the epitome of England; whatsoever is excellent in the whole land being found in proportion thereto ... Beside God hath been pleased to make it the birthplace and nursery of many great men.' (Cheers.)

George probably had a penny or two under the bed or wherever he kept his brass. There were some rich people but we must also remember the grey ranks of the poor. The rich were always scheming how to get more. It was eventually called capitalism. When they decided that the commonland was a wasteful way of organising the countryside, they had the idea of enclosing the commons and dividing up the land among interested parties. So the Enclosure Acts were introduced and with the passing of every act another tract of common land was walled round so that the new owner could develop farming without the intervention of the rural riff-raff, who used to own it.

The poor and humble folk, having lost their ancient rights to use the land, now had to work for their 'betters'. Some of the dispossessed still had a bit of spirit left. A man who was hauled before the bench for stealing a goose was asked what he had to say in his defence. He replied: 'If I go to jail for stealing a goose from off the Common, what will happen to those who stole the Common off the goose?'.

The Yorkshire landscape was tamed, acquiring a gridiron pattern of walls. They look attractive now, especially to rabbits, rats, snails and sheep wanting a bit of bield (shelter) on a stormy day, but some writers of the time of the Enclosure Acts thought they were a monstrous intrusion on the landscape. A wall is really two walls in one, each wall bound to the other by big stones known as 'throughs' and with capstones for durability. The raw material came from the outcrops and crags. Norman Nicholson, the poet, talked about walls walking on stone hoofs. They do move, incessantly, as they settle down, but if well-built they keep their shape for a century or more.

The walling tradition continues to this day. A Wharfedale farm man recalls:

A lot of t'stone was aw right. You did get odd parts where t'stone was'nut all that good. Sandstone stuff (we called it 'greet') was not bad to wall wi'. So was a lot of t'limestone if there were sharp bits on it. You got a lot of shapes and sizes, but they fit in wi' one another. You wanted 'em rough-edged so that they would bite in. Limestone, though in many cases it was smoother than sandstone, played heck wi' your fingers. I knew a fellow as worked wi' us walling limestone up in Wharfedale. He walled till he was leaving red fingerprints on t'stone. We said: 'Now come on, give ower.' But he were there next day. He was a hard man.

Some stuff we used at Hazelwood and Storiths looked as though it had come out t'river bottom. It was hard stuff, like granite. It'd been smoothed over wi' watter at some time. You try and wall wi' them things – oh, man! I put a gap up for an owd-fashioned farmer – by gum, he was an owd stager – and I'd a heck of a job to make it stand. I told him it was bad stuff to wall wi'. He said: 'Thou mun excuse me for saying so, Geordie, but it looks as though t'damn pigs have bin at it.' All I could say was: 'If thou gets any pigs near this, it'll be down again.'

Towards the end of the eighteenth century, the Industrial Revolution gave some shrewd and enterprising Yorkshiremen a chance to make money from muck. The woollen industry was primitive, which suited those who drew their livelihood from it, including the handloom weavers, sitting at their looms in the upper storeys of their houses, looking out over sunlit fields and nipping out of doors when it was time to milk the cow or have a chat with the neighbours. At any given moment, wool in various degrees of processing was being moved along the old tracks on the backs of packhorses.

Some inventive people mechanised the old hand processes. There were ruptions from the old hand-workers, but you cannot stop progress. Soon the handloom weaver, who was his own boss, had become an employer, working all hours for next to nowt, getting grey-faced with fatigue and spitting out mill-muck when eventually he staggered home for a few hours sleep. When things had been 'shakken out', as we used to say, the worker was marginally better off than he had been. Being your own boss, and facing slumps as well as boom times, is the quickest way to t'graveyard. The new-style bosses got others to do their worrying for them.

The West Riding was well placed for industrialisation. Here were moors, yielding soft water in the form of becks and rivers. The humidity of the air helped the textile processes. Also handy was one of the country's biggest coalfields. Millscapes appeared and chimneys belched smoke. The triumphal establishment of milldom meant that a host of workers were soon packed into back-to-back housing thrown up in a hurry, without much regard for sanitation. Sulphury-yellow sunsets were the norm except during Wakes weeks, when the fires were put out and all who could afford the fare went to the seaside and coughed the soot from their chests.

Middlesbrough, by the Tees, was a Victorian creation, devoted to heavy industry. Sheffield boomed as a steel town, benefiting from a new type of furnace invented by Henry Bessemer. Night became day as the blast furnaces were kept operating, meeting the high demand for best-quality steel. Yorkshire seemed to be set in a ring of fire.

Pits were opened up. Barnsley (known to the locals as 'Barnsla') became identified with coal and also for the appetites of its menfolk. A hungry man might fix his teeth on a Barnsley chop – a mutton chop, weighing anywhere between three and four pounds. Blue scars became badges of honour to those who could be persuaded to spend their daytimes in the ill-lit, dusty confines of the mines. Not all blue scars were to be classified as industrial injuries. Samuel Cheesbrough, of Kippax, told of a Yorkshire miner with such a scar who told an enquirer: 'Wife was frying bacon; it burnt and she hit our young 'en. I told her that if she hit him again, I'd hit her. So she hit him. I hit her. She hit me – wi' t'frying pan!' (Read it slowly, several times, for maximum effect.)

The first wave of mill and factory owners were paternal, though the houses thrown up by so-called jerry-builders in the early days were damp and cramped. Yorkshire thrift was evident at the home of a mill-worker who, when a friend called, was scraping off wallpaper. The friend asked him if he was decorating. The mill-worker replied: 'No, lad – we're flittin'.' The them-and-us age of industrial relations began when the workers, feeling they were being exploited, banded together to fight for better conditions.

Leeds became renowned for its multitudinous activities. Or summat like. As with other industrial places, literally tons of soot fell over the buildings and the populace. A Leeds professor was to discover traces of distinctive local chemical deposits on the mosses on Malham Cove and even on trees in the Lake District to the north-west. Traffic increased, leading to a need for wider streets. One man, who had difficulty in crossing, shouted to a man on the other side, enquiring how he got there. The man replied: 'I was born here.'

Life was cheap in nineteenth-century West Yorkshire. Funeral stories proliferated. The wife of a mill-worker, who had been pensive for a while, remarked: 'I've just been thinking, Fred – if owt 'appens to awther on us, I'll go and live in Morecambe.'

Fred replied: 'If I'm ever buried, it'll be on top o' thee.' The 90-year-old couple were walking sorrowfully from the cemetery after burying their son, aged sixty-five. The man said to his wife: 'I telled thee we wouldn't rear him.'

The narrow Pennine valleys became packed with canals, roads, mills, terraced housing, Co-op stores and chapels. You could tell the chapels from the mills because the windows were arched. The building line reached was far above what, in normal times, anyone would consider laying bricks and mortar. Everywhere got a thin film of soot. The moorland sheep were grimy. The sparrows coughed. The lungs of the weavers filled up with fluff. It didn't really matter. There was no such thing as sick-pay. If someone went off sick, there was always someone else needing a job. If someone was late for work, the maister had the pleasure of docking a penny off the wage.

Although few people were aware of it at the time, the textile industry and others had peaked in about 1860, which was the time when cities and towns, in a surge of civic pride, built huge town halls. The wealthy industrialists gave parks (to be named after them) in which the workers could get some fresh air and recuperate before turning up for work at first light on Monday morning. Leeds, Bradford, Middlesbrough, Sheffield and others were now big and bustling places. By 1880, Hull had become the third largest port in Britain.

A vibrant period, the world's first great industrial revolution, was to have its ups and downs. Today, the textile industry is automated. The output achieved by hundreds in the old days is attained by a handful of well-paid operatives. Farmers, now mechanised, still have to run to stand still if they want to make any brass.

The old-time ranks of the workers were thinned by war. In the First World War, the east coast was bombarded by the German navy. The inter-war years were marked by industrial unrest and a terrible trade depression. In modern times, with a movement from manufacturing into white-collar industries, Leeds has become the major administrative area.

We still glory in our food, for it's your stomach 'at 'ods your back up.

God bless us all an' mak' us able.
To ate all t'stuff what's on this table.

Whatever it might be.

4 Yorkshire Speech

E's double-fisted an' threpple-throited [throated].
[Said of a boozer.]

Reet, then! Just remember tha's in Yorksher, not York*shire*. And that just as tha doesn't chuck thee brass about, so there's no need to be liberal wi' words. Arnold Kellett, a prominent member of the Yorkshire Dialect Society, gives as an example (of so little, meaning so much) the two words 'Nay, lad!' They might be the equivalent of: 'I'm very disappointed in you, son. I thought you would have been able to do better than this.'

When a Leeds telemarketing company – whatever that is – announced it was looking for the authentic voice of Yorkshire, there were titters all the way from Sedbergh to Spurn Point and from Whitby to Waddington. There are dozens of authentic Yorkshire voices. Stanley Ellis, who has made a lifetime study of Yorkshire dialect, commented: 'There is really no such thing as a Yorkshire accent.' Another devotee, Arnold Kellett, urges us to beware of imitations!

To test out the multi-accent theory, go for a long car ride and stop every few miles to ask the way. You'll be capped (surprised) at the differences between Halifax and Morley, West Riding, North Riding and East Riding. Stanley Ellis, when asked about the quest for *the* voice, instances the pronunciation of the word chicken which, in Morley, is spoken as though it had an 'r' before the final 'n'. Six miles away, at Hyde Park, the version is 'i' before the 'n'.

If an 'off-comed-un' were to have a crash course in Yorksher dialect, then he/she would have to remember certain key words, to be used or understood when they are overheard. A Yorkshireman doesn't earn money; he 'addles' it. Use 'allus' for always and 'summat' for something. If someone says: 'I'll be blowed' or 'I'se fair capped', it means they are astonished (or 'sore amazed', as the good book has it). If you're hungry, then you're 'pined'.

If somebody remarks that they'll finish a job 'if I'm owt like', it means he'll have to be feeling on top form before he tackles it. Stand in a bus queue down Barnsley or Dewsbury way, and you are aware of local pockets of dialect and, sometimes a Chinese quality about the language which is not pure dialect – nor, indeed, especially Yorkshire but an example of sloppy English: 'Whowhoshewi?' (Who was she accompanied by?).

'Shewowiahsue' (She was with my sister Susan).

Practise some basic West Riding dialect by reciting 'Ilkla Moor'. Take a hammer and flatten your vowels. The Yorkshire accent of the south-west is, in essence, broad. Repeat a few key words such as aye (yes), ay! (really?), owt (anything), nowt (nothing), 'appen (perhaps), abaht (about), and knaws, as in 'tha knaws' (you know). Clip your speech, to save time. Tha's bahn up t'street, not up the street.

In Yorkshire, use Ah for I and remember that if you are setting off on a mission you are 'getting agate'. If you can't afford a washing machine, you'll need a posser [a pole with a copper head] for agitating the clothes in soapy water. Don't confuse the posser with a possit (hot drink) or a porriwiggle (tadpole). Whatever happens, don't waste words. The classic business conversation, between a visiting traveller and a manufacturer, runs like this: 'Morning.'

'Morning.'

'Owt?'

'Nowt.'

'Morning.'

'Morning.' Be racy, especially when trying to get a bargain. Offer a bob [shilling]. Hear the other man say he'll cap thee by giving ninepence. Then tell him you'll cap him – by taking it!

Crack a joke. Especially one concerning sheep or wool. An impatient motorist, following a flock of sheep along a narrow road, and seeing how the several men and dogs were having to fight for control of the flock, wound down the window of his car and asked: 'Who is the master of this flock?'

An exasperated farmer replied: 'Yon little black-faced 'un at t'front.'

The media tends to go for its Yorkshire personalities to an area south of Leeds where there's a glorious mish-mash of accents resulting from the boom years of coal mining, when thousands of families from all ower t'shop were sucked into villages which sprang up like mushrooms in a summer pasture. The mining families were said to keep their coal in the bath and the men did not wash their backs because it was debilitating. Folk'll say owt. The area did prove to be a good breeding ground for cricketers, among them Fred Trueman and Geoff Boycott.

I was born at Skipton, an unhappy meeting place of West Riding and East Lancashire accents, resulting in something hard and flat. We were truly 'by gum' types. Skipton was said to be the gateway to the Dales. But once a traveller crossed the watershed beyond Buckden, the dale country was inhabited by folk who had a different sort of speech. Examples were provided by John Thwaite, the Wensleydale dialect writer, when he recorded a hayfield attack by midges:

> When t'midges land than t'neck yan wipes
> An' [hay]reeaks er dropped an' fooak leet pipes.
>
> Hoo [how] t'lile beggars mak tan scrat,
> Midges allis see te that!
>
> Neea shakkin' off, neea good te pleean,
> They help thersefs te fat an' lean.
>
> T'owdest worker – sixty, mooar,
> Nivver knew 'em wass [worse] afoor.

Arnold Kellett, an authority on dialect, says that the old Celtic language survives in Yorkshire only in topography, as with the names Penyghent, Chevin, Calder and Nidd. The Romans did not stay long enough to convert the natives to Latin. (Years later, the toffee-nosed Normans fared better in this respect). The Angles, a hard-working lot from north-west Europe, had a kingdom called Northumbria – north-of-the-humber – and their speech remains the basis of that in the North and East Ridings. Danish Vikings sailed up the Humber, captured York and established thirdings (Ridings).

The Norse-Irish were comparatively few in number but left lots of names for places (such as Keld, Thwaite and other villages in Upper Swaledale) and names of natural features – fell, dale, tarn. They used the word laik (to play). When, many centuries later, a motorist asked a man in a depressed industrial area the way to the Lake District, one of the out-of-work who was consequently laiking replied: 'Tha's arrived!'

When the Normans took over, there were two tiers – the nobs speaking French and the ordinary folk still laiking. The two coalesced and were sanctified by William Caxton and his printing press. This made some Yorkshire folk perversely stick to their dialect and write it down – though it was much easier to hear it spoken than to have to wade through a solid mass of bits of words with a scattering of apostrophes and the occasional 'reet'.

The softer speech of the east means that how becomes hoo. Which can be confusing, as when a visitor to Whitby, having got into conversation with a fisherman, asked: 'And who are you?'

The reply was: 'Aw – nobbut middlin'. Hoo's yoursen?' The word middlin', meaning moderate, and applied almost exclusively to health, is capable of being used with fine shades of meaning. A man who had been reported as being middlin' said, when asked about his health: 'Nay, I doubt I'm nobbut just middlin'.'

John Byass, of Bridlington, who often preached in Methodist chapels in the old East Riding, was able to lapse into the local dialect at a moment's notice. He told a story of how a congregation of three – woman, child and a man hard of hearing – were present until he was about to announce the text for his sermon. 'Then t'lahtle bairn began ti whimper, so t'woman ups an' taks it oot.'

If you fancy your chances with the native speech of north and east, try reciting this excerpt from a book called *Goodies*, twenty-three tales written by Walter F. Turner which in the less bustling days of long ago kept people entertained with wit and humour. H.L. Gee selected one and 'ventured to trim the dialect so that the rank and file in and beyond Yorkshire may enjoy this colourful glimpse of the old days'.

Here beginneth the words of Walter Turner:

It fair caps me 'at folks want ti eat goodies in choch. Yan wad really think some folks couldn't say their prayers wivoot a goody. It caps owt. T'parson on Sunday had nobbut just started service when a fat owd woman in t'front o' me thowt she wad hav a goody; an' she began scrattin' aboot ti see if she could find yan, an' she kept on scrattin' while we gat ti t'Psalms.

She knawed she'd left tow or three goodies fra last Sunday, else she wad hev getten some mair when she war in Pickering; but noo she couldn't find yan, neither a mint nor a acid drop nor an aniseed nor owt. Hooiver, she wor desperate jealous she owt ti hev a goody iv her pockit somewhere, so in t'fost lesson she begins to tak all things oot of her pockit – an' what a vast o' things that there woman had, an' what a tewin' an' twistin' she had ti get at a bit o' goody 'at worn't there!

Ah couldn't fairly tell what there wasn't in that pockit. Ah just shut mi eyes an' oppened 'em again, an' Ah thowt Ah wor at a jumble sale instead of at choch. There wor t'door key. There wor a anketcher. There wor a button-hook, a kettle 'odder, fower or five bits o' band, a thimmle, a pin-cushion, a yard measure an' arf-a-dozen 'airpins becos she oppened 'em oot – she thowt t'goody had mebbe getten among 'em. Oh, an' there wor a bit o' pencil wi' a brokken point, an' a bit o' wax an' a deal mair things. They wor all i' yan pockit.

Turner described in amusing detail how the old lady replaced all the objects. She leaned back in the pew to have a rest. Then, just as the parson began his sermon, and had given out the text:

she had ti gan tiv her pockit again. She dives in an' catches hod o' t' anketcher bi t'corner an'rives it oot, an' thimmle [thimble] flies oot wiv it, an' rattles ower t'seat ... an' a goody tummels oot o' thimmle!

Ah nivver seed neerbody si pleased. She wor fair capped was t'owd woman. She popped t'goody intiv her mouth – an', by gum, it wor a mint, an' desperate strong an' all. It fair reeked all ower t'choch; an' there she sat knappin' an' knappin' till she stuck a bit in a corner of her cheek to make it last. She listened ti t'sermon mebbe a minute an' then she started scrunchin' away again ... an' efter that she took oot t'thimmle ti see if there wor onny mair goodies in, bud there weren't. [Here endeth the abridged lesson].

An old poem about a Wensleydale lad's visit to Leeds and his first entry into a church is recorded in verse. There were 'thirty or forty folk, i' tubs an' boxes sat, when up cooms a saucy owd fellow. Says he, "Noo lad, tak off thi hat" '. Finally:

When preachin' an' prayin' were over, an' folks were gangin' away,
I went to t'chap i' t' topmost tub. Says I, 'Lad, what's to pay?'
'Why, nowt,' says he, 'my lad.' Begor! I were right fain.
So I clicked hod o' me gret club stick, an' went whistlin' oot again.

On the Wolds, a lad at school was taken to task by his teacher for using a word in a sentence which should not have been there. Teacher asked him what was wrong. He pondered for a while, and replied: 'Ah've gone an' putten putten wheer Ah owt ti hev putten put.'

Out in the west, Emily Brontë, who had an Irish father, a Cornish mother, and an imagination which must have kept her awake at nights, grew up at Haworth surrounded by people who thought they were talking proper but were using dialect. Emily did not dilute it to make it more intelligent to the general reader. Listen to Joseph, the servant in *Wuthering Heights*:

'Whet are ye for?' he shouted. 'T' maister's dahn i' t' fowld. Goa rahned by th' end ut' laith, if yah went tuh spake tull him.'

'Is there nobody inside to open the door?' I hallooed responsively. 'They's nobbut t' missis; and shoo'll nut oppen 't and ye mak yer flaysome dins till neeght.'

Yorkshire dialect was being widely spoken by the bulk of the population at the time of the Brontës. It was in the West Riding that numerous regular publications – annuals and almanacks – fixed the character of local communities in a way which was cheap in price, lively in concept and with a pawky humour which appealed to the grey mass of the people, who led weary lives in mills and workshops. Reading dialect (as opposed to hearing it spoken) can be tiresome, but many of these annual publications lasted through to the beginning of this century.

John Hartley's dialect poems entertained generations of Yorkshire folk, and especially Ahr Mary's Bonnet:

Es-ta seen ahr Mary's bonnet?
It's a stunner an' nooa mistak!
Yoller ribbons, yoller rooases,
An' a gurt big feather dahn t'back;
Ahr Mary went ter ch'ch last Sunda'
T'congregation did nowt but stare;
T'parson says. 'This is nut a flahr-show,
But a house of prayer';
Ahr Mary says: 'Thy 'eead's bald,
Nowt in it, ner nowt on it:
Would-ta like a feather aht o' t'back o' my bonnet?'

At Slaithwaite, in textile country, a mother was concerned that her son, on his way home from the mill (sometimes a little worse for drink) might fall in and drown. She said: 'Ah, lad, Ah'm fane to see thi', but o'm fair flaid ut tha'll be coming whoam draended some neet.'

The son said: 'Ah' mother – oh'm flaid o' shall.'

Mother remarked: 'If tha does I'st nivver get ovver it.'

And the son replied: 'Nur me nawther.'

At a Co-op store in West Yorkshire, an owd chap asked: 'Hev yu onny leeters?'

The assistant enquired: 'Litres of what?'

The old man's caustic reply was: 'Fireleeters!'

At Halifax, a pensioner, weary of listening to a conversation between his wife and one of her friends, said: 'Gie us key, lass; I'll be get'n kettle on 'till thee gets 'oame.'

Down at Doncaster, two sisters were reconciled after a serious disagreement. They met in the bedroom of one of them who was dying. Said the sufferer: 'T'doctor says Ah'm boon to dee. 'Appen he's reet. If Ah do, tha maun unnerstand tha's forgiven. But mind, if ivver Ah'm up an' aboot agen, things stop as they were!' An old friend who liked the good life, and spent freely, said that his last words, uttered when someone raised him up on his death-bed, would be: 'Ah'm bloody skin't.'

Arnold Kellett concludes that real 'brooad Yorksher' is in decline. People are more outwardly mobile. Yorkshireness has been diluted by off-comed-uns, the invaders from other parts of England. What chance does it have against sloppy telespeak and the horrors of American English? Yorkshire speykes keep alive the virility of the old Yorkshire speech. The slim woman was said to be 'as thin as a lahtle bit o' soap after a lang day's washing' and the fat man was said to be 'carryin' all afore 'im'.

W.J. Halliday, a Yorkshire dialect authority, recorded these three examples of Yorkshire speech: (1) A gooid way to stop a chap's maath is to keep yer awn shut. (2) A chat 'at's liberal wi' advice is generally niggardly wi' brass. (3) Them 'at hez nowt is nowt – if they'd bin owt they'd have 'ad summat.

Many new terms used in country areas relate to tractors and cars. Years ago, when cars were still something of a novelty, a West Riding farmer testified in a police court case involving a car. A magistrate asked him what sort of a car it was, only to be told: 'Nay, I don't knaw.' Then, suddenly inspired, the witness added: 'It wor one o' them pip-pippin' sort.'

5 Some Tribal Customs

Marsden, wheeare the' put t'pigs on t'wall ter listen ter t'band.
[Told of a West Riding village – and doubtless others.]

The nearest we Yorkshire types come to an annual get-together is at the Great Yorkshire Show, which after a nomadic existence was eventually sited near breezy Harrogate. You can usually tell a Harrogate man because as he approaches a corner, he holds his hat on. Harrogate is virtually a bouquet of flowers. Blooms are everywhere during the warmer months. It's astonishing to find such floral beauty at an elevation of six hundred feet.

The 'Great Yorkshire' is a distillation of the rural life of the county, with stock-judging, produce of all kinds, trades, crafts and a grand parade of the prize-winners. Visiting farmers and schoolchildren make directly for the tractors and machines, ransack the leaflet stands and, on windy days, contribute to a blizzard of paper. A York man, looking somewhat sad, remarked to his neighbour that he had been thinking of going to the show but – 'you know how it is: congestion on the road, nowhere to sit when you get there, and if it is not pouring down it's too blooming hot.' Said the neighbour: 'Aye, I know how you feel. My wife won't let me go either.'

Show talk is fast and loud as families 'catch up' on the gossip. It's a form of stocktaking (six months later, the despatch of Christmas cards is the equivalent of a second profit-and-loss account concerning relatives and friends). At the show, there can be quite a racket, to use an old word which J.B. Priestley used in one of his Dales stories, told in the 1930s. He referred to the farmer's wife who every week went shopping in Kettlewell (normally a quiet village). When she stopped visiting the shop, and someone enquired the reason, she said (succinctly): 'I can't stand t'racket.'

On my last visit to the Great Yorkshire Show, a friend who had been laughing loudly during a conversation with a farmer near a particularly noisy piece of machinery told me: 'Ah nivver heard a word he said – but 'appen it was summat likely!' I shamelessly eavesdrop on old farmers. A conversation opens with 'How do?' or something amusing like: 'By gum – Ah thowt tha were deeard!' Another conversation began with what a stranger would take to be offensive but, in the context of Yorkshire farmers, was affectionate: 'Na then, you miserable owd bugger.' A classic, told to me in Nidderdale, was of the farmer who asked a friend about his wife, to be told: 'She's a little angel'. When the other farmer asked the same question, the first man replied: 'Mine in't deeard yet.'

One showtime conversation related to a sheepdog. 'I can't mak my new dog see sense,' said one.

'Its nae better then?' remarked the other.

The owner of the feckless dog said: 'Nae better? It's bloody useless – at least ten times nae better!'

Another time, a farmer was ranting on about the laziness of modern youth. 'I told my lad that in t'owd days I thowt nowt o' gettin' out o' bed at five o'clock, and do you know what he said? He told me he thowt nowt on it either!'

There's a wash of homely talk around the stock rings. It's mainly about the quality of stock but now and again someone finds time for a tale, such as that of the farmer who decided to take over from his shepherd when it came to picking the next tup for the flock. The shepherd, his pride dented, was determined not to like any tup the farmer picked. When the farmer returned and stood the animal in the yard for inspection, the shepherd said nowt. 'It's got a pedigree,' said the farmer, blusteringly.

''Appen so,' said the old shepherd, adding: 'And Ah've nivver seen a tup more in need o' one.'

Perhaps it was the same veteran who, when told he would be provided with a lady assistant, said: 'The last time I heard of a woman doing a job like this, she made a mess on it.' Who was she? Said the shepherd: 'Bo-Peep'.

The show programme begins with Otley in the spring and ends with the autumnal Nidderdale show, its venue at Pateley Bridge (or Patela', as the natives call it). I had the pleasure, in 1995, of helping with the compilation of the centenary brochure, known as 'Pateley Rant'. Local people provided a fund of stories and a torrent of pictures. My favourite tale was that of Parson Wright, Vicar of Pateley from 1931 to 1949. Each year, he bought three dozen 8-week-old pullets from a farmer at Wath.

One of the pullets, some weeks later, had grown a large comb and developed an unusual crow. He complained to the breeder, who duly exchanged the offending bird. This went on to develop into a fine specimen of Rhode Island Red Cockerel, which the breeder duly entered in a class at Pateley Show. The cockerel won its class. Parson Wright, visiting the poultry tent, heard the bird give its peculiar crow and immediately recognised the prizewinner as the bird he had turned down earlier in the year!

County players were among those taking part in show day cricket. In the centenary brochure is a story of when Maurice Leyland was fielding on the boundary. A farmer who had been imbibing began to shout uncomplimentary remarks about the play. The ball came out towards the boundary. Leyland ran to field it. The comments went on. Leyland dropped the ball, just in front of the moaning farmer, who shouted: 'Nay, Leyland. Ah cud hev copt that wi' mi gob!'

Maurice Leyland replied: 'And if I'd got a gob as big as thine, I'd have had no trouble catching it!'

Village cricket thrives, with moments of high drama. In a local match, one team batted miserably. The other team fared little better and in due course were down to their last man, with the scores level. The bowler hurled down a ball which passed the wicket some three yards wide. The match had been won. One of the losers asked the bowler if that last dismal ball had slipped as he was about to deliver it. 'Nay,' he replied, 'but I wasn't going to let that chap have t'pleasure of scoring t'winning run.'

The Yorkshire year is peppered with quaint communal customs, a whole cluster of them being centred on Easter. Before the festival arrived, Collop Monday was observed with gifts of collops (slices) of ham or bacon. On the following day, Shrove Tuesday, pancakes and fritters were made and Morley rang what became known as t'pancake bell. On Good Friday, Pennine communities were visited by mummers, who performed a pace egg play, concerned with resurrection and the triumph of good over evil. Dr Buck, of Giggleswick, a friend of the composer Elgar, researched the local version of this play.

Some of the Eastertide celebrations were energetic, an example being skipping on the foreshore at Scarborough on Shrove Tuesday. Traditionally, it is for people of all ages and their hard physical efforts are rewarded at lunch-time with a gargantuan meal, featuring bacon, eggs and pancakes. Also at Scarborough, Eastertide saw the making of Simnel Cake, the name related to a type of bread used in spring fertility rites in Ancient Rome(!). It was usually produced on what is now known as Mothering Sunday. I believe the reason for making this cake was so that servant girls, given a day off on the fourth Sunday in Lent, customarily visited their mothers with a gift.

As they have long said in Yorkshire: 'It's thi stomack as 'ods thi back up!' The Easter tradition at Whitby was playing shuttlecock in the streets, which is no longer possible now that visitors' cars are so common. Baked custard, made with milk, sugar, eggs and grated nutmeg, was served to the children. If an easterly wind was blowing at Easter – and this is often the case – it was described as a custard wind.

Custard was a nice basic food enjoyed by Yorkshire farmers who didn't care for 'owt fancy' and when at the auction mart tended to suck strong mints. One of them described trifle as 'ower many tastes at once'. A dish at a café which looked sickly and clarty prompted the retort: 'Ah've nivver eaten stuff like this, but Ah've often trodden in it.'

Easter was the time when Yorkshire mothers poured noxious liquids down the throats of their offspring to enliven the blood and to fortify them for a range of street games. Young, athletic West Ridingers clambered out of bed in the chilling darkness and set off to walk to the summit of Beamsley Beacon to 'see the sun dance' at dawn on Easter Sunday. Nowadays, Good Friday is the main walking day or, for the less energetic, is the day when the new car is taken out for a spin.

Yorkshire folk are united in a love of good food, especially roast beef and Yorkshire pudding. Traditionally, the beef was reared in a Yorkshire pasture, where the summer grass grew hock deep. The pudding was made at the last moment when the beef fat in its tin was heated until it smoked. When the batter was added, a loud sizzling was heard. Yorkshire pudding waited for no man. It was man who waited for the pudding, which was eaten as a first course for lunch on Sunday.

In Yorkshire, nowt goes amiss – not even dock leaves. I am not referring to the type of dock which, providentially, grows where there are nettles and is an antidote if a person receives nettle-stings. Growing on riverbanks in the Calder Valley is *Polygonum bistorta* and at Easter many of the leaves are plucked to make dock pudding, which is not much to look at but could be relied on in spring to cleanse the blood. Children who had a bad attack of bronchitis at this time were taken to where roadwork was in hand. The children, smothered in clothes, were made to stand in the tarry vapour and inhale the fumes.

My wife is the only person in the history of Yorkshire who has turned down the gift of a brace of grouse. I had taken a countryman deer-watching. He turned up at the door with the grouse as the ultimate thank-you offering. Most people would have accepted the gift, whether or not they liked grouse. A friend who was born with a silver spoonless mouth, and who has never owned a grouse moor, dresses for dinner on the Glorious Twelfth (opening of the grouse-shooting season, a day which is inglorious for grouse) and he opens a tin of grouse breasts. Over at Cowling (or Cowin'eeard, as the natives call the village) the Glorious Twelfth is referred to as the Quack, and those freeholders with moorland rights exercise them, including the shooting of grouse, most of which are refugees from adjacent, well-keepered moorlands.

The grouse is said to have a peaty taste. The nobs hang it and have it served with added flavours to kill the natural taste. Though the grouse feeds well in late summer and autumn, when not only the bonnie heather blooms but the cloudberry, otherwise known as the 'mountain strawberry', puts forth its orange berry. The person who looks for cloudberries on the high moors has unfair competition from the resident grouse.

Turkey is now high on the Yorkshire menu. It is a matter of Yorkshire pride (there's that word again!) to note that a Yorkshireman introduced the turkey into Britain. Young Strickland, of Boynton Hall, near Bridlington, sailed to Newfoundland with Sebastian Cabot and saw wild turkeys. He collected some when returning home. Go into Boynton Church today and you will be reminded of this when looking at the lectern. For instead of the traditional brass eagle, there is a cock turkey, carved in wood.

The thought of a pint of Yorkshire-brewed beer arouses acute nostalgia in exiles the world over. One of several famous breweries was established at Tadcaster in 1758 and was taken over in 1847 by the Smith family, Samuel Smith acquiring it for his 24-year-old son, John, who developed it mightily, drawing the hard, clear water from a well which is still in use. New premises, built in the 1880s, crown the Tadcaster skyline. It is said that a man who staggered into a local inn on a very hot day requested: 'Two pints, please. A pint 'ud nobbut wet one side o' mi throoat.'

The chapel has been a considerable social force in Yorkshire affairs for almost two centuries. Years ago, the chapel folk, abstaining from strong drink, had their love feasts, when there was fervent prayer, moving addresses and feasting on basics – water and bread. When summer outings were planned by the chapel folk, one of the delicacies was scripture cake, so named because the ingredients were to be found in the Bible and they were presented with regard to the Biblical texts, an example being 'four and a-half cups of Kings iv, verse 22', which was flour.

The established Church also had its social occasions – and its scripture cake. The worship was somewhat less emotional than that of t' Methodists, Baptists and Congs (Congregationalists). Sometimes it might be downright tedium, as on an occasion when, at an evening service in a parish church, only the vicar and verger remained. Eventually, when the vicar showed no sign of ending a very long sermon, the verger approached him and left the keys on the side of the pulpit, whispering: 'Wilt ta lock up when thou's finished?'

Clerics produce flashes of humour. Twenty years ago, I asked Donald Coggan (then Archbishop of York) for his favourite Yorkshire story. He recalled an informal moment when he was Bishop of Bradford. His wife and he having been out for a country walk, they were casually dressed and he wore an old pair of grey trousers and an open-necked shirt. When they came to a little shop, Donald Coggan poked his head round the corner and asked: 'Any crumpets?'

The lady behind the counter called out to her husband: 'Albert, do you want any crumpets?'

He called back: 'No thanks – not today.' The bishop and his wife did not get their crumpets, but 'we did get a good laugh'. When John Hapgood, Archbishop of York, retired in 1995, and was asked what advice he might have for his successor, he replied: 'Don't try to be me ... And I've left instructions on how to work the boiler.'

On at least one occasion, in remotest Yorkshire, in the days before radio ensured our time-keeping was accurate, the vicar turned up at a church to find the few parishioners hard at work in the hayfields. 'Thoo's come a day too soon,' said one of the men. The vicar insisted that it was Sunday. Another man, after reckoning up, counting fingers, said: 'Vicar's reet, lads. Let's get on wi' t'service.'

In Yorkshire, cricket has been elevated almost to the status of a religion. Some unusual variations have been recorded, including an annual tradesmen's match in Ilkley, when one team wore black hats and the other donned white hats. Elsewhere, a match has been played every Boxing Day, regardless of the weather.

Freddie Trueman, who amassed 307 test wickets, tells of an immaculately clad varsity skipper who was dismissed by the first ball and congratulated the bowler on his delivery. 'Aye, it were a good ball,' said the Yorkshireman, 'but not worth getting dressed up for!' A visiting batsman who congratulated a Yorkshire bowler on getting him out first ball was told: 'I wasted it on thee!' Yet another bowler, who was wearing his coat, disappointed the crowd.

Someone shouted: 'Buck up, lad – tak thi coit off.'

The bowler shouted back: 'Ah've nivver takken me coit off to work and I'm not going to start takking it off to play.'

Golf now has its fanatical following. Yorkshiremen like to take on the Scots on their own ground, and particularly at St Andrew's, where one man from the White Rose County found himself bunkered and made several frantic attempts to get clear. The Scottish caddie watched with an expressionless face. Said the Yorkshireman, flustered for the first time in his life: 'Golf's a funny game.'

The caddie replied laconically: 'Aye – but it isna meant to be.'

Two Leeds men were playing on the Temple Newsam course and the poorer player held up the game by a succession of fruitless shots. He said: 'I'd move heaven and earth to play golf well.'

His partner sighed and remarked: 'Nay – keep on trying. Tha's only heaven to move now.'

At Giggleswick, they have an ebbing and flowing golf course. It lies almost in the shadow of a limestone scar, which for centuries has attracted travellers because of its ebbing-and-flowing well caused, it is thought, by a double syphon in the rock. When the golf course was brought into use just over a century ago, the magazine *Golfing* described it as being 'eminently adapted for golf, as the turf is of excellent quality and natural hazards abound'. These took the form of 'hillocks, rocky mounds and cliffs, intersecting walls, roads and, last but not least, a mountain beck, which by its serpentine course, traps the hapless ball of the unfortunate foozler.'

Two years later, *The Golfer's Guide* mentioned numerous hazards, including 'roads, paths, walls, ditches, sand-bunkers, streams, steep rocky prominences, etc., etc'. The ebbing-and-flowing effect noticed in the well has also extended to part of the course, where a tarn once lapped and fretted. One February day, the lower part of the course mysteriously flooded to a depth of two feet six inches. Yet four days later the water had ebbed and the land was capable of being played on.

Until recent years, the members shared their course with cattle, sheep and even geese. The greens were wired off so that the cleaves of farm stock did not churn up the surface. If a ball didn't go in t'beck, it might lurk – cryptically coloured – in a patch of daisies. Among the perils were cow-claps, leading to the inclusion of this item in the rule book: 'A ball finishing in dung may be lifted and dropped no nearer the hole.'

Yorkshire has long been renowned for its horses. The best horses, bred in the limestone country of North Craven, had good bones. Among the hoary tales of horseflesh is that concerning the man with an ailing animal who asked a friend what he might do about it. 'I gave my poor horse paraffin,' said the friend. The two men met again a month later. The first man remarked: 'I gave my horse paraffin – and it died.' Said the second: 'So did mine.'

Yorkshire horse-dealers were known for their shady practices. Jonty Wilson, blacksmith, used to tell of Brough Hill Fair, in Westmorland, which was patronised by many from the Yorkshire Dales, observing that it was wise to have made a mistake in every aspect of horse-dealing before tackling the sharp dealers of Brough. One man who took a white horse bought a black horse and, on getting it home, found it was his former animal – blackened!

Farmers returning home in horse and trap were invariably 'market fresh' but continued to call at any public houses. At one, while the farmer was at the bar, some local youths took his horse out of the shafts and put it back the wrong way round. The farmer, contemplating the strange sight when he left the inn, eventually concluded the horse had thrown the trap over its head.

George Borrow wrote: 'Shake a bridle over a Yorkshireman's

grave, and he'll rise up and steal your horse.' A somewhat gruesome ballad, Clapham Town End, deals with haggling between two Yorkshire dealers, one of whom is offering a horse which has died and the other a horse which is on the point of death. In the end, they swapped. The dead horse having been skinned, its purchaser fared worse than the other man. He was better off 'by a skin and four shoes'.

The aforementioned Dr Buck, of Giggleswick, collected the words of the ballad and also the air and passed them to his friend Edward Elgar who, much against his will, for he preferred original composition, harmonised the music, sending it back to the doctor by return of post, as though he couldn't bear to have it on his desk. Elgar and Buck, who met when they were young men, untramelled by matrimonial ties, had a common interest in rural life, in animals – and in what the Victorians called japes – irrational but diverting pastimes. Once, when visiting Giggleswick. Elgar and his friend kidnapped Miss Buck's parrot and bore it off, cage an' all, to Settle. As they crossed Settle Bridge, the bottom fell out of the cage and a bemused parrot was left on the pavement.

Elgar in later life was fond of backing racehorses. Indeed, when his memorial service was held in Worcester Cathedral, there was a pewful of jockeys, each one saying what a great man he was! Our Yorkshire racecourses have long histories and draw vast crowds. An old friend of mine said: 'Betting's a fool's game'. He added: 'The last time I backed a horse, it came in last. I should have noticed the jockey was carrying a thermos flask and some sandwiches.'

Racing has been known since, in Roman times – according to Sir Theodore Cook, in his history of the turf – the Emperor Severus Alexander enjoyed the spectacle of horse-racing and kept his Arab horses at Netherby, near Wetherby. Kiplingcotes has had a racecourse since 1519, and on the third Thursday in March the horses race for prize money based on the interest on brass left for the purpose some four centuries ago. Middleham and Malton are two places where horses are trained for the turf.

Angling has produced a rich crop of stories, many of them by T.K. Wilson, of Skipton. Brass bands include Black Dyke, associated with the huge mill Queensbury, on the roof of the West Riding. H.L. Gee told the story of a famous brass band which had a diminutive drummer. He was so small he could not see over the drum. The band was marching through the town when, at a fork in the road, the band turned left and the drummer went right. A friend shouted to the solitary musician that his pals had gone the other way. He replied: 'Doan't fret thissen. Ah knaw t'tune.'

The classic tale of a West Riding band concerns one which, returning in triumph from a competition at the Crystal Palace, in London, disembarked from the train and decided to play themselves into town. It was after midnight. One of the bandsmen thought it best if they took off their shoes so that they wouldn't wake up the local folk.

In summertime, the brass bands played at seaside resorts and in the parks of towns and cities. It was a time when tribal activity took place outdoors, as described by a Victorian poet living in Leeds:

> The joyful Sabbath comes, that blessed day,
> When all seem happy, and where all seem gay,
> Then toil hath ceased and then both rich and poor,
> Fly off to Harrogate or Woodhouse Moor.

Harrogate was a noted spa. Medicinal waters had been discovered as early as 1570 and in the following century it was written that the waters here 'cheereth and reviveth the spirits, strengtheneth the stomach, causeth good and quick appetite and furthereth digestion'. The several wells eventually attracted royalty, and Harrogate became even more fashionable when the Royal Pump Room was built in 1913. A Harrogate schoolboy, asked what God does, said: 'He saves our Gracious Queen.'

Woodhouse Moor at Leeds was where local crowds gathered for outdoor attractions. A quack doctor produced bottles of pick-me-up and also several lemons. He squeezed a lemon until it no longer dripped and, on opening his hand, revealed a lump of mush. 'If anyone can get another drop of liquid from this lemon, I'll give him five pounds. And, friends, you'll all want a bottle of the stuff which made it possible.' A diminutive man came forward. He grasped the remains of the lemon and squeezed. Nothing happened for a while except that the veins stood out on his forehead. Then, to everyone's surprise, a few drops of liquid fell to the ground. The amazed salesman asked the little man what he did. He replied: 'I'm a Church treasurer.'

Prominent among the tribal customs in Yorkshire is the Burning of Owd Bartle at West Witton, in Wensleydale. This hygienic disposal by flame of the effigy of a sheep-stealer may be something much deeper – a fertility rite, indeed, though I do not want to shock the old ladies of the dale by going any further into that aspect. One of them told me: 'I don't think they should make all this fuss about a sheep-stealer.'

A story of Bartle's theft of mutton-on-the-hoof has been put about, but does the Wensleydale ceremony go deeper? Is it an echo of scapegoat practice. Are the West Wittoners unwittingly placating the old pre-Christian gods? Or are they keeping alive the old and once widespread story of a ruffian (under many names) who gets his come-uppance at the hands of the local folk?

The cremation of Owd Bartle takes place at Bartholomew-tide, which is at the end of August. The effigy is borne through the village at the head of a procession. It is then put to the torch (or match) amid much jollification. There's some old doggerel to recite. It helps if the reciter has had a few pints of ale to drink to enable him to lose an inhibition about making a public spectacle of himself, for dalesfolk are normally quiet, even shy. The verse recalls the last hours in Bartle's life:

> At Penhill crags he tore his rags,
> At Hunter's thorn he blew his horn,
> At Capplebank stee he brak his knee,
> At Grassgill beck he brak his neck,
> At Wadham's End he couldn't fend,
> At Grassgill End he made his end.
> Shout, boys, shout!

The church at West Witton is dedicated to St Bartholomew, which may (or may not) be significant. An old Wensleydale friend with a deep knowledge of English sports and pastimes links Bartle with St Bartholomew's Fair, which was abolished in various parts of the land because of its rowdiness.

At Whitby, on the north-east coast, a hedge is planted – on a muddy beach not far from Boyes' Staith. Known as the Horngarth, or Penny Hedge, it is assembled on the Eve of Ascension. The custom has been going on for over eight hundred years. Doubtless when it began the participants worked with bare feet. Now it's a welly-job, performed by members of the Hutton family. The ceremonial includes the blowing of a horn. The origin is as vague as Bartle, with some delightful stories to choose from. A garth is a yard or enclosure fenced with wood. The Horngarth appears to be a survival of days when a horn was blown to summon the homagers and tenants of the Abbot of Whitby to repair the hedge annually.

Belief in the supernatural is not a strong part of Yorkshire lore. The Queen of the Fairies is supposed to live in a snug cave beside Janet's Foss, at the head of Malhamdale. In a record drought during the summer of 1995, the cave was fully exposed and people ventured into it, reporting that nothing which might conceivably have belonged to a fairy could be seen there. Perhaps Janet or Jennet is more closely associated with the witch-cult, and a fairy, complete with wand and ballet dress, would soon look grimy and bedraggled if she strayed anywhere near what is normally such a wet and mossy place as the Foss. When the Hon. John Byng, during a horseback tour of the North in 1792, visited the cave, on his way to Gordale Scar, he wrote in his diary that fairies once inhabited the area but 'are now quite out of fashion'.

In the Dales, they thought more about the barquest, a spectral hound with eyes as big as saucers or the headless horse which had been reported from Camhouses – presumably while looking for its head!

There's nothing Yorkshire folk like better than a good funeral relating to someone who has lived long and well and has provided not only for his/her relatives but the funeral guests as well. A wedding is a solemn event but everyone can relax at a funeral when the dear-departed has, indeed, departed and those who knew him gather at a hotel or tearoom for refreshments, a custom which takes the chill from the joints (if the funeral has taken place in winter) or stopped the rumbling stomachs of those who have travelled afar.

The Revd J.C. Atkinson, whose fascinating book *Forty years in a Moorland Parish*, relating to the North York Moors, was published in 1891, mentioned funeral cakes being served. They were sometimes known as funeral biscuits. Atkinson noted that when a Dales freeholder had been buried, the mourners went for a meal and found that between two and three hundred-weight of meat, mainly beef and bacon, had been set out for them. Even more food was available when the deceased man had been the owner of one of the inns at Castleton.

It is said that a dying Yorkshireman detected the smell of ham being cooked and requested a piece. 'Nay,' said the wife, 'we're cooking that for thi funeral.' A Yorkshirewoman who was widowed when her husband 'dropped down dead' was asked the cause of death and replied: 'It's one o' them funny illnesses, where you don't knaw thou's gone till it's happened.'

6   Along the Coast

Steeas yackers, flither-pickers, herrin' guts fer garters.
[Uncomplimentary reference to Staithes –
a flither is a limpet, used for bait.]

To the seaside farmer, or to a fisherman about to launch his boat into the short, sharp sea which laps against North-east Yorkshire, the weather is a dominant topic. At the start of every day, a man taps his barometer with the gusto of a woodpecker at a nesting tree in spring. The best weather is to be found on picture postcards. Look at rows of cards outside a souvenir shop, and you'd never imagine the Yorkshire coast is beset by such a depressing condition as roak – a sea-fret, damp and chilling and so thick you can taste it.

An old tar I met on Whitby quay recalled when t'roak 'was that thick if we 'adn't knawn where we were, we wouldn't 'a knawn where we were'. Another seafarer, emerging from the damp greyness of early morning, said: 'Ah reckon t'day must hev bin up aw neet.' I have visited Whitby when sunny conditions prevailed to within half a mile of the coast but the coastline itself was swaddled in vapour, robbing me of a view of the celebrated red roofs, a myriad orangy-red pantiles – a futuristic pattern against the blue of harbour, sea and sky.

Sometimes the clearance of the roak is swift, dramatic, like a transformation scene at a pantomime. I climbed to Whitby Abbey on a day when I could just see a hand in front of my face. The moaning of the Hawsker bull (a foghorn) deepened my doleful mood. Then the mist dispersed, rising like a curtain, revealing all with clarity and colour. The old town by the Esk luxuriated in hot sunshine.

A northerly wind, non-stop from the Arctic, bombards a coastline which, in the Whitby area, runs east-west. In the blast, keel boats bounce on the waves. The gulls are grounded. It is said that the skipper of a keel boat who was fighting to keep it t'reet side up prayed: 'Oh, God, send down thine only son to save us.' His companion added a postscript: 'Nay, God, cum down thisell. This is noan a lad's job.' The blue-ganseyed fisher folk have a stoical acceptance of bad conditions. On a stormy day, when I joined one of them in the lee of a building, he commented: 'We're having a bit of a blaw [blow].'

On sunny days, the north-east coast of Yorkshire gleams and crescent-shaped bays are flecked with silver light. Sand, not estuarial mud, is a feature of the north-east coast. Spray shooting up from Filey Brigg, a line of dark rocks extending far out to sea, gives the Brigg the appearance of a spouting whale. The rocks were said to have been positioned by the Devil, whose grand plan was to extend the barrier right across the North Sea. He slipped and on falling grasped a haddock, leaving fingermarks on the fish, as you can see to this day. Who says the Yorkshireman lacks romance?

Eighteenth-century fishing villages huddle, as though for mutual warmth, at Saithes, Runswick Bay and Robin Hood's Bay. Further south, at Bempton and Flamborough, a line of chalk cliffs gleams white, early and late on a summer day, when the sun is upon them. The ledges teem with seabirds, from the droll little puffins to Omo-white gannets. A visitor to this and some other bird-favoured parts of the Yorkshire coast is likely to trip over a birdwatcher. When I first visited Bempton, men were still being lowered from the cliff-top to collect eggs, an ancient pastime which was soon to be legislated out of existence. Now Bempton has a showbiz flavour, with a proper carpark, wardens, colourful publications on sale and warning signs galore. Some of the best bits are fenced off, to protect the birdwatcher, not the birds.

When I took an artist to Bempton – he, poor lad, had been in hospital for heart surgery and I wanted to put him where the smell of anaesthetic would be blown away – he sat down and did a lightning sketch of an albatross. I looked through the host of circling, shouting birds but did not see one of the huge birds which sailplane in the southern ocean. 'But you've never seen an albatross,' I remarked.

'Does it matter?' he replied. 'Some o' t'best artists have painted angels.'

At North Landing, Flamborough, cobles – the inshore fishing-boats of this coast – look like colourful seals which have hauled themselves from the sea to sun themselves. Many years ago, before the tourist boom, I quizzed a Flamborough farmer about his land. He told me of the various crops and the acreage they had been allocated, adding: 'And I've half an acre of caravans; it's worth more than the rest put together.'

Artists abound on Flamborough Head, where the owner of an eighteenth-century cottage was asked by a professional painter if he might 'do' a water-colour of it. The owner was keen to know what would happen to the painting. It would, said the artist, be exhibited in a big city. The owner brightened and asked: 'Will you put a notice on t'picture so folk will know I rent t'place out i' summer?'

The flow tide booms against the cliffs. The ebb tide retreats with its mouth full of boulder clay. Someone got a perverse thrill from mapping the existing coastline and marking in lost villages on what is now the North Sea. The erosion is at its most spectacular on the Holderness coastline, which is composed entirely of boulder clay. A great dollop of newly eroded clay, with boulders set in it, looks like Grannie's pudding-mix. The khaki tide jettisons much of its load of silt at Spurn Point.

This lightning tour of the Yorkshire coast is so sketchy I must fill in some details. If I had a favourite place overlooking the grey North Sea it would be Robin Hood's Bay, where the buildings now sit primly atop a concrete cliff. It is a pity the designer did not leave a few ledges for the gulls. They now festoon the local chimney pots and sound Reveille as, ten minutes after dawn in summer, a wash of grey spreads across the sky at the onset of a new day.

On parts of the Yorkshire coast, the sun leaps out of the sea, as though anxious to get everyone motivated for another day's work. One of my favourite fishermen used to say: 'T'day begins when my bare feet touch the bedroom room.' He didn't like to see his wife ligging in bed too long. 'When I make her a cup o' tea, I stir in half a teaspoonful of Epsom's Salts. It's not long afore she's jumping oot o' bed.' A few touroids enjoy walking at first light. They see the last of the night shift – a few rod-and-line fishermen who have fished the ebb tide, collecting fluke and codling. The last full-time fisherman of Robin Hood's Bay walked into the history books many years ago.

Visitors patronise the fish and chip shops. I'm told that a man who went into a shop beside the quay in Whitby asked for 'fish and chips twice'.

The man behind the counter quickly replied: 'I heard you first time'. (At a fish and chip restaurant in a Yorkshire city where the fish was not always fresh, a customer asked for 'fish and chips – and a kind word'. He got his fish and chips. He reminded the waitress he wanted a kind word. She whispered: 'Don't eat the fish.')

Visiting the Yorkshire coast, fifty years ago, I took the service train from Pickering to Whitby, reached a town which in its homeliness was more like a glorified village, then went by train or bus down the coast, chatting *en route* with blue-ganseyed fishermen at the tail-end of a long tradition. The lives of the Yorkshire inshore fishermen were ruled, in part, by superstition, which regularised their behaviour.

At Whitby it was considered unlucky to wind a ball of knitting wool after sunset. A Filey woman with a grocer's shop would not sell any eggs after the sun had gone down. At North Landing, Flamborough, a fisherman baiting a line would stop work at once on hearing mention of a pig. If, in grandfather's day, when a few large fishing boats operated as far as the Dogger Bank, anyone went on board a yawl with a pin stuck in his coat, he had to throw it overboard immediately.

In the days of small boats and big seas, death stalked the fisher folk. The gansey (blue knitted jersey) worn by all the fishermen varied in style according to the place where it had been knitted. So if a body was pulled from the sea, the origin of the dead man was quickly established. If a fisherman or woman died at Filey, the relatives pulled down the blinds of their windows. A death in Queen Street led to virtually every house being blacked out, for there were large and interconnected families, especially Jen-kinsons, including Laffy, Tich, Tin, Bonzo and Buggins. Members of the large Camish family were nicknamed Chicken, Tutor and Miser.

They knew the Yorkshire coast almost as well as the tiny parlours of their homes. Visitors were at a disadvantage, but did their best in emergency. When a holidaymaker reported the loss of his wife's watch to the police, he specified a certain place just off Filey Brigg. The policeman asked him how he could be so sure about it. Said the visitor: 'That's where she fell in.'

A visitor to Bridlington, asked why he had left his wife at home, said: 'She'd been to Brid afore.' I hope he did not stay at the farmhouse-cum-bed and breakfast place where rabbit was served at every meal. On the Friday, the farmer bounced into the dining-room and said: 'You'll be waiting for your rabbit pie.'

One of the guests said, flatly: 'What we need is a bloody ferret.' The coast is geared to tourism. Day-trippers arrive by coach, from which they descend asking for toilets and afternoon tea. Not all the visitors are quite sure where they have been set down. An old lady I met at Filey explained, ruefully: 'I could be anywhere. I slept all the way here.' An all-male party from a club usually has a few crates of beer in case they develop a thirst on the way to the coast.

In pre-railway days, the little fishing communities were isolated, having the sea before them, the moors behind and roads of indifferent quality connecting them up. They had a splendid setting against which to enact their lives. Boulby, just north of Staithes, is (at 666 feet) the highest point on the east coast of England. It's best to dress up for a walk to the top, for there's usually a draught from the sea. A young woman who staggered up there in a mini-dress was rebuked by a local man, who told her: 'Thoo should wear more than that. It looks not much bigger than a pelmet.'

Old Staithes (pronounced Steeas) is pincered by cliffs. The road to this old fishing village is doonbank and so steep you have a fancy you might look down some of the chimney pots. Every other roof has its squawking gull. Dame Laura Knight, one of the celebrated Staithes group of artists, called Staithes 'a wildified place'. At the edge of human memory, fishwives from Staithes – many of them wearing a distinctive type of bonnet – made an early morning visit to villages up to nine miles away, going from door to door, carrying clothes-baskets of fish, calling their wares as they went. A man who accompanied them had the main stock of fish on a special cart.

The ghosts of fishermen and smugglers are said to roam through the village. Perhaps, also, the sensitive visitor hears the fishermen's choir, which was said to be so good, 'they could sing a piece oot o' t'*Darlington and Stockton Times*'. In a superstitious age, villagers claimed to have seen waifs (spiritual doubles). One day, a person might turn a corner in the village and meet his or her waif – face to face – looking it straight in the eyes and chanting: 'Waff, Waff, gan thee weeas, an' deean't coom 'ere no more.' The waif would then disappear. As an old Quaker friend remarked, when unconvinced: 'They'll say owt!'

Runswick Bay is the name for an indentation on the coast and also of an old village where most of the houses were set on a sloping ground. The carpark is on a steep slope. Visitors double-check their brakes before leaving their cars. A friendly hob, ligging in a sea-cave, has a reputation for curing whooping-cough. The mother of a child suffering from this ailment would take the child to the cave and call out for assistance. Nowadays, with the National Health Service, the Runswick hob is suffering from neglect.

Whitby, on either side of the tidal Esk, has extensions to its piers which resemble the claws of a lobster. St Hilda, who founded a cliff-top Whitby Abbey, rid the district of its snakes by cutting off their heads and turning them into stone. At least, that is how local people explained the presence of fossilised ammonites, an extinct type of shellfish, which can be found in the cliffs and has given a boost to the tourist trade. Ammonites featured (as three coiled serpents) on the coat-of-arms of the towns, whose (somewhat lame) motto is: 'We Were and We Are'.

Way back in 1849, Whitby was reported to have a summertime invasion of folk who admired 'its venerable Abbey, its magnificent iron-bound coast scenery, as well as to enjoy the fine saline-bathing, redeem health and drive away care, by a cessation of their accustomed avocations'. The west cliff was developed between 1848 and 1860. It was then that the Khyber Pass (!) was cut through solid rock to connect the west pier with the new estate.

Whitby is a breezy, colourful, friendly place. A statue of Captain Cook (a Cleveland lad) shows him gazing over the old town and the sea. Whitby might have seen the birth of a great evangelical movement, called the Salvation Navy rather than the Salvation Army, the name eventually adopted. During a coast campaign at Whitby, in 1878, the title of 'captain' was used, to appeal to local fishermen. If the campaign had continued, more nautical titles would doubtless have been selected. The military titles were adopted because they had general appeal.

The *Whitby Gazette* takes second place to the Bible on the bestseller list. It is said that a Nonconformist preacher began his prayer by saying: 'Oh Lord, as thou wouldst have seen in last week's *Gazette* ...' A Methodist minister who returned home mentally whacked told his wife he had been trying to convince an out-of-town congregation it was the duty of the rich to keep the poor. His wife asked: 'Did they accept it?'

Said he: 'About half of 'em. I convinced the poor.'

The old God-fearing fishing community would have been appalled at the (modern) tourist hype concerning Dracula. It is a pity that Bram Stoker, while staying here in the late 1890s, should write his novel *Dracula* and have the famous count shipwrecked off Whitby, where he takes the form of a large dog and goes to ground in the grave of a suicide victim at St Mary's. The Celtic saints like Hilda once kept paganism at bay. Now the Dracula cult has let the demons return and helps to keep the cash registers ringing. A young television presenter recently introduced an item on Whitby in a holiday programme. She went in search of Dracula, standing in the churchyard after dark. An actor dressed up as Bram Stoker's weird creation cavorted in the background. Alas, poor Whitby, what have tourism and television done to you?

When I first saw Whitby, the graveyard was also a vantage point from which to see the sun set over the sea. Ice-cream eating was not allowed in church. Camping was prohibited in the churchyard, as if anyone is likely to do this! Whitby, with its busy harbour and blue-ganseyed fishermen, consumes colour film by the mile. A visitor shakes his/her camera, thinking it has jammed. Yet another film has been used up. A photographer's wife collapsed on the quay. One of his friends asked him what he had given her. He replied: 'Fiftieth of a second, at f11.'

In the days before the stock of North Sea herring was decimated by over-fishing and pollution, the Scottish fishing boats joined the locals at the height of the season and it was possible to walk across the harbour, moving from deck to deck. Some people fished from the pier. A holidaymaker hired tackle, was given some bait, cast the line and waited for nearly an hour for summat to happen. When the line went taut, he drew out a splendid flatfish. The angler threw it back, saying to his neighbour: 'I don't fancy that fish – it's bin trodden on.' At Whitby, everyone chuckled at a harbourside notice: 'No fishing for children'.

The inshore fishermen of Yorkshire had enormous pride in their family links with the coastal towns and villages. At Whitby, a visitor chatted with a fisherman, who began to recall the generations of his family who had gone to sea in ships. The visitor said: 'You'll be telling me before long that your family sailed with Noah.'

The fisherman snorted and replied: 'My family's always had its own boat'.

In Victorian times, the jet industry was booming. Jet is a glossy black fossilised wood. It has been valued, carved, polished, since the Bronze Age. Lumps of jet are found on the local beaches. They made attractive ornaments at the time when the Queen was in mourning and, for many years, the national colour was black. Two men discussed jet. One of them remarked: 'It's powerful stuff.'

Said his friend: 'How do you make that out?'

The first man replied: 'They're running aeroplanes off it now!'

Over thirty years ago, when the fish quay was open to all, I'd cadge a lift on a keel boat sailing the following morning and then, at an early hour, arrive on the quay. I was usually far too early. Sixpence coaxed coffee from a machine which also retailed hot chocolate and oxtail soup. One of Whitby's small salmon cobles would pass, its white hull gleaming in the artificial light from the town. 'Queer things, salmon,' said a young fisherman as another coble went silently by. 'They can smell the rain, you know. They lie at sea, waiting for a freshet ...'

The last time I went to sea from Whitby I was in the keel boat *Galilee*, which had three 'fleets' of lobsterpots to inspect – 280 pots in all. There was much talk about lobsters, 'them damn lobsters – they're like tortoises and sleeps when it's cold'.

I have a special fondness for Robin Hood's Bay, where romantic tales are told of smuggled tobacco and spirits such as brandy, which were passed from one house to another without appearing in the open air. I heard of coffins being lifted through landing windows, which was easier than taking them down a constricted flight of steps.

One day, when the steps were being used to convey the body of a particularly caustic housewife, a clumping sound was heard from within the coffin. The lid was removed. The 'dead' lady sat up. She was quickly revived and lived a few more years, continuing to keep the household in order with her waspish tongue and aggressive ways. When she died, the body was placed in a coffin, which was on view in the bedroom according to local custom. On funeral day, the coffin was being borne down the constricted stairs. Said the widower, anxiously: 'Go easy, lads ...'

The spirit of the place was caught in several books by Leo Walmsley. His book *Three Fevers* was filmed as *Turn of the Tide*.

The fevers were – lobster, salmon and cod. Leo grew up in an area where life was largely governed by the restless surge and ebb of salt-water over the scaurs. He was to recall a boyhood encounter with what he took to be a salmon – a real salmon, with silver scales, caught when wading among the scaurs. Local men laughed at his claim that this large fish was a salmon. They laughed – but did not mock. One of them thought it was a grey mullet. He'd caught one in his salmon nets years ago. Captain Bunny identified it as a bass. He'd never seen one caught in these parts before. 'And fine eating they are, too – better than a salmon.'

Several shops in Robin Hood's Bay sell second-hand copies of the Walmsley books and also the several new editions of his work. In his book called *Phantom Lobster* (a title which Leo later considered to be unfortunate, as it made many think it was either a ghost story or a thriller) he told what happened when he returned to Bramblewick (his name for Robin Hood's Bay).

On my last visit to Robin Hood's Bay, I awoke to the bugle call of a herring gull. Baytown, viewed from the top of the bank, was a dense grouping of buildings roofed with red pantiles, the whole protected from the sea's pounding by a concrete cliff. I began a knee-cracking descent of the steps beside Bay Bank until a notice offered me the option of walking via the sea wall. The council path had the usual local government 'furniture' – a bollard, seats and litter bin.

The grassy space where I now stood would, in olden times, have been a mass of housing. During the last two centuries, no less than two hundred dwellings have slithered down the cliffs.

Among the buildings claimed by the sea was the studio of Dame Ethel Walker, an artist who died in March, 1951. Baytown has been so attractive to artists you had to step over them. Dame Ethel's studio was described as 'clinging to the treacherous cliff by, here and there, an obstinate claw buried somehow in the solid rock'.

Down at the cobbled Wayfoot, as a somewhat cramped landing place is known, I realised again the limitations of Baytown as a fishing village. Fishing was a local occupation in the sixteenth century, when a visitor described the place as a 'fishchar tounelet of 20 bootes'. Boats approaching Baytown have had to negotiate a channel between two boat-ripping scars.

When I visited Major Will Lacy at his house, The Coble, at the sea's edge, he showed me the living-room windows, set at a slight angle so as to deflect the rumbustious waves. Said Will:

It can be a bit nerve-wracking when a wave thunders down on the terrace above the living-room. In really wet spells, the water drains down the cliff slope from Cow Pasture Hill and the whole slope becomes a soggy bed of water channels and mud, slithering down to the shore, to be washed away by the tides.

Baytown is (to quote Will Lacy) 'an almost perfect example of an eighteenth-century village'. Most people know it only during the warmer part of the year. In winter, when many of the houses are empty, their owners snug in towns and cities, a north-easterly wind puts ice crystals in the blood. It piles up the sea, which breaks its back, with an explosive thud and shower of spray, against a concrete cliff. People did seem to 'wear well'. A new doctor, having examined a lively octogenarian, proclaimed there was nothing wrong with her. She exclaimed: 'Nowt wrong. I was in failing health before you were born!'

At Ravenscar, the cliffs have a maximum height of almost 600 feet. On one stretch, 100 feet down is an enormous undercliff, or Beast Cliff, which varies from 150 yards wide to 30 yards. Below there is a steep drop to the rocky beach. No roads approach it. The few paths are so steep and difficult they are rarely attempted. The undercliff is wild with bracken, bramble, bushes and stunted trees. There are sinister pools and bogs. It is a resort of badger and fox. Adders sun themselves on the rocks.

Elsewhere, a farmer and his ploughman were carting sand from the shore when men who were at a local rifle range opened fire and the ploughman dropped, exclaiming: 'I'se shot!'

The farmer scrambled up the bank, waved his hands at the shooters, and demanded: 'Stop that shootin'. Ye've shot a man. It could easily have been t'horse.'

The persistency of sea-fret (the dreaded roke) would have something to do with the abandonment of a grandiose scheme for building a holiday town at Ravenscar. The place was laid out with broad streets and sites for shops. It had been originally known as the Peak but when the railway came it was re-named Ravenscar.

Little of the old venture remains but here, at the Raven Hall Hotel, is the termination of the forty-mile Lyke Wake Walk, devised by Bill Cowley. One of the sights, usually in the late afternoon, is the arrival of walkers, teenagers and stone-agers, limping, listing, sun and wind-tanned and with puffed or blistered feet. Sometimes, in an emergency, a visitor has to be plucked off our Yorkshire moors by helicopter. A walker, seeing one hovering for ten minutes, said to his companion: 'What a nuisance. I bet he's run oot o' petrol.'

There are two Scarboroughs – North Beach and South Bay – separated by a headland where the remains of a castle stand like ancient molars on a gum of green. The connecting road, Marine Drive, is in the shadow of Castle Hill where thousands of kittiwakes, which are oceanic gulls, turn up during the nesting season and cross the drive, spattering cars and causing a small percentage of holidaymakers to carry out some surreptitious dry-cleaning. When the kittiwakes are back at sea, and the north-east wind gives the tide an extra punch, sheets of salt-water wash down the road and pavements, making it undesirable for the open-topped double decker buses used during the season to continue in service.

North Bay is the one where the roke establishes itself if weather conditions are right. The impression is that a grey curtain has been lowered at a theatre. South Bay, which has the best beach, is generally crowded in the season, with any refugees seeking the open air Suncourt at the spa. Peasholme Park has a Japanese flavour with its pagoda, waterfall and Oriental-type lanterns. Twice a week, during the summer, naval battles take place on the lake. At other times, rowing boats criss-cross the lake like big water-beetles.

Food of all kinds is available. Diehard Yorkshire folk go for the specialist dishes – the local scallops, Whitby kippers and (fanfare, please) Yorkshire pudding. A visiting journalist was a little unkind to the fish and chip shops when he wrote of fried food being 'typically northern: greasy and flaccid'. And he 'wouldn't give you tuppence for most of the pubs, which smell of stale smoke and play awful music …'. A comment which applies generally.

An old man, recalling the start of the 1914–18 war, tells of a local Methodist preacher who prayed: 'Oh, Lord, them Germans is at it agen.' He paused, and added: 'Skidaddle 'em, Lord, skidaddle 'em.' Scarborough was one of the places bombarded by the German Navy. Two men took refuge behind a boulder. One remarked: 'Dizzn't tha think we'd better pray?'

The other replied: 'Ho'd hard a bit – let's see what happens first!'

Tobias Smollett (1770) had indulged at Scarborough in the new craze for sea-bathing, which gave the town a claim to be Britain's first seaside resort. The bathing machines were ranged along the beach, each a small, snug, wooden chamber, fixed on a wheel-carriage, having a door at each end. On either side was a little window above and bench below. The bather entered by wooden steps and shut himself in. Here he undressed. If he was ill or weak – sea-bathing was considered beneficial in both cases – there was room for an attendant.

As the potential bather undressed, a horse was yoked to the end next to the sea, drawing the carriage forwards until the surface of the sea was level with the floor of the dressing room. The horse was then fixed to the other end. The person within, being stripped, opened the door to seaward, where he found the guide ready, and plunged headlong into the water. After bathing, he re-entered the chamber by the steps (shifted for that purpose) and put on his clothes at leisure. The carriage was drawn back again on to dry land.

Scarborough has its late-season cricket festival at which, on a sad occasion, a visiting batsman trounced the Yorkshire bowling to the extent of hitting the ball to the boundary – using one hand only. A hard-bitten Yorkshire spectactor remarked to his pal: 'Bah gum, lad – yon begger's played afoor!'

Cricket is a feature of the life at many local villages. At one match, where the ground was by no means as firm or level as that at Scarborough, someone hit the ball so hard it went down a rabbit hole. The batsmen kept running. Forty-four runs had been obtained before the ball was back in play. The captain – told, in an audible whisper, that he should have shouted 'lost ball' after the visiting batsmen had run six – said: 'It wasn't lost. It were just that I couldn't reach it.' The match resumed. In due course, the demoralised captain was out for a duck.

A spectator grunted: 'Ah think he'd be better employed mowing t'nettles.'

There's nowt like a week or two on the Yorkshire coast for acquiring a tan or a brownish hue which (if there has been a sea-fret) might be analysed as rust. Stephen Fewster, who used to be publicity manager at Scarborough, told of an old Pudsey chap who had been ill for some time but, when he was on the road to recovery, was sent to Scarborough by his doctor for a week's convalescence. The sun shone every day. Alas, towards the end of the week, he suffered a relapse and died. His body was taken back to Pudsey. The relatives gathered round his coffin, paying their last respects and consoling the widow. His sister turned to her and said: 'Ee, lass, but he's a lovely colour – that week in Scarborough did him a world of good.'

Filey, in its lovely half-moon shaped bay, extends a finger of oolitic rock – the celebrated Brigg – so far to sea that those who walk along it have the joy of seeing wild waves on two sides of them. Filey folk were so superstitious they would have nothing to do with religion. In 1806, preachers who came from Bridlington were pelted with plaice and dried skate which was so hard it drew blood. Johnny Oxtoby introduced Christianity. He said that sooner than give the place up, he'd live on 'cauld taties and sleep on a booard'. He did not have to do it for too long. Soon the first chapel had been opened ...

Flamborough was known as Little Denmark. For centuries, once a year, an arrow was shot seaward in the general direction of Denmark, as fealty to the old regime. Flamborough fishermen used donkeys for transporting equipment or the catch of fish from the village to either north or south landing. There would be about a hundred donkeys in the village and two men tented them (cared for them at a charge, which was a shilling a week per donkey, all the year round). Donkeys were notoriously stubborn. A man who had struggled with a donkey for half an hour during the journey back to the village with a load of fish met a pillar of t'chapel and asked: 'How did Noah manage to get two o' these animals into t'Ark?'

Bridlington, beside its half-moon shaped bay, which used to be thronged by coastal shipping when a gale was blowing, reminds me of the time I had a minor motor accident and asked a local garage proprietor to patch up the car so I could make the trans-Yorkshire journey home without any part of the car dropping off. He told me: 'These repairs'll cost you more than you think – and that's just an estimate.'

I was told of the exacting working conditions of fisher folk and then 't'credit side' – pubs open from six in a morning to eleven at night. 'If you put a tanner on the bar counter, you could have a pint of beer, an ounce of bacca, box of matches and a clay pipe. Aye, an' t'clay pipe was put into t'beer to tan it.'

Holderness, a triangle of flat, fertile ground in the south-eastern corner of Yorkshire; is bounded on the west and north by the Wolds and to the east and south by the North Sea and the Humber. The land is morainic debris – sand, gravel, clay – carried from distant places by the ice sheets. It erodes swiftly, prompting a local farmer to say: 'Man's just a lump o' clay. A woman taks him an' maks him into a mug.' During the 1939–45 war, a shocked and bleeding crew member crawled out of the wreckage of a German plane and came face to face with a Yorkshire farm-hand. The German, hoping for sympathy, indicated he was wounded. Said the farmhand: 'Well! Thoo shun't a cum!'

The Spurn peninsula, between the Humber estuary and a sea which has the same khaki hue, gives Yorkshire a dramatic termination. Spurn is virtually held together by a road which extends to where a few lifeboat men – the only paid lifeboat crew in the country – are handy for emergencies on one of the busiest estuaries in the country.

Spurn is a nature reserve. Every other person has a pair of binoculars hanging from the neck. Birds come in all shapes and sizes, from the brent geese (refugees from the Arctic) to 'little brown jobs' in the bushes. Here, as well as anywhere, you become aware of the seasonal ebb and flow of life as birds commute to and from their northern nesting grounds. At Spurn, where Yorkshire ends in sand, shingle and marram grass, where the sea is in constant battle with the river under a big sky, a visitor inquired from one of the few locals: 'Whatever do you find to do down here in winter?'

The reply was: 'Same as i' summer, but wi' us overcoats on!'

7   North York Moors

Yattoners wade ower t'beck ti seeave t'brig.
[Of Great Ayton ('seeave' means save).]

Yorkshire's north-eastern moors, which sprawl across a thousand square miles, are thatched with heather. Three species – bell heather, cross-leaved heath and ling – form a low shrubby layer over peat which is moist and brown, like fresh chocolate cake. Stir it up, as with the boots, and it becomes distinctly clarty. The heather provides both food and shelter for the stubby-winged grouse, a bird which has plenty to grouse about.

At a thousand feet or more, springtime is usually a little late and can be a time of snow-flurries or stinging frost. The hen grouse covers her chicks like a feathered tea-cosy. If the chicks survive into summer, they may be short of food as a drought frizzles the vegetation and dries up those boggy areas where the birds usually feed. With the moors tinder dry, a cigarette smoker can cause havoc by tossing away his fag unstubbed. A good moorland fire rages for weeks on end if it sets the peat smouldering.

Having endured much, the grouse must then fly through a hail of shot from the sporting types with their tweeds, green wellies and Range Rovers. For a few days they exhibit all the symptoms of moorland rage and then their temperature comes back to normal. By November, the cock birds are again claiming territories. The cycle of new life and violent death repeats itself ...

The heather also helps to sustain the horned sheep, which are Blackfaces or Swardles (Swaledales). Mostly they stay on the moors, but now and again – like the proverbial chicken – they decide to cross a road. Motorists stand on their brakes.

Sometimes, a collision is inevitable. A dead sheep lies where it falls and the body attracts our Yorkshire vultures – the carrion crows and magpies.

The adder, Britain's only poisonous snake, slithers through the mini-jungle and does its best to avoid humans. Otherwise, the Moors are user-friendly. Especially in late summer, when the ling is in bloom and there is a horizon-to-horizon carpet of imperial purple. The upland roads are thronged by motorists out to enjoy the sight of what Stevenson called the 'vacant wine-red moor'. The uplands do not have a universal appeal. A West Riding man, at the end of a journey organised by his daughter, was asked for his thoughts and commented matter-of-factly: 'There's nowt but scenery!'

Even the scenery vanishes if there is mist or a blizzard. The last time I experienced such conditions on the Moors was in the merry month of May, when I followed the trackbed of the old Rosedale mineral line, looking for the Lion Inn at Blakey, where I was to spend the night. The weather had been behaving itself that day. Then a snowflake landed on my nose. A wind sprang up from nowhere. In minutes, the snow was so thick it blotted out the landscape.

Thoughts of a big open fire in the old moorland inn sustained me for the last half mile. And next morning, as I looked out of my bedroom window, to see the Moors silvered by hailstones, a ring ouzel (which I normally think of as a bird of the wilderness) arrived to collect a few worms from among the wooden tables set out for visitors. I set off along the road to Blakey Ridge, standing for a few moments before a rough boulder inscribed to the memory of Frank Elgee, historian of the Moors. Frank had a host of moorland recollections.

Frank told of an August day in 1912, at Fen Bog, when he pointed out a slow worm (a snake-like creature) to 'a gentleman, a lay-reader, a Sunday school teacher, a teetotaller, non-smoker, and instructor of the young. To my amazement, he most ferociously attacked the inoffensive reptile, battering it on the head with his stick until it was lifeless.'

On to Ralph Cross, between Castleton and Hutton-le-Hole. The North York Moors Park chose this old moorland marker as its emblem. He is strictly speaking Young Ralph, to distinguish him from nearby Old Ralph. No one will confuse him with another local cross, Fat Betty, especially as Betty has been whitened and looks as though she died of shock.

Young Ralph is supposed to have succumbed to a blizzard. The first celebrity to face the fury of a blizzard on these moors is said to have been William the Conqueror, who was on his rounds after his victory at Hastings. When I paid homage to Young Ralph, the countryside creatures were still numbed by the sudden violent storm of the day before. The road verges were littered with the bodies of bumble bees. Ralph is tall and seems to be standing on tiptoe, as though wanting to make the most of the clear-weather view of the North Sea, away to the east.

I eventually crossed Glaisdale Moor, in the heart of the National Park, following an ancient track, which looked half as old as time. Curlews called. A merlin, the smallest of our falcons, went by, looking for 'little brown jobs' – meadow pipits and skylarks. I looked into Great Fryupdale, and sniffed the air, half-expecting the tang of bacon being cooked.

Keeping pigs was a popular Dales occupation. The local pig-killer was busy, especially in the autumn, when he might be assisted by a younger man. The pig-killer returned later, when the meat had cooled, to cut it into handy pieces. It is related that at a moorland farm, his helper was making such a bad job with a cleaver that the worried pig-killer said: 'Go easy, lad – or you'll get both lugs (ears) on yan side.'

The North York Moors are in Jurassic terrain, laid down some 150 million years ago. Visiting geologists talk glibly about Lower Lias and Upper Oolites (which are the entire Jurassic sequence). Glaciologists enthuse over the effect slow-moving ice had on the landforms. Naturalists become secretive if anyone mentions the rare May lily. Motorists either glory or shiver nervously when the byroad they have been following makes an abrupt descent of a moor-edge or, winding, delivers him/her to a ford, where the water may be axle-deep.

> On this hill three becks are born
> Through the ribbed limestone they have worn
> Three channels. How their waters purl,
> Eddy and ripple, tumble and swirl!

Ice from the Vale of York, pressing against the western edge of the Moors, ensured there would be no drainage from the high ground in that direction. Pressure from Scandinavian ice, which came up against the coastal or eastern side of the Moors, blocked the mouth of the Derwent, which – though rising within six miles of the sea – had to find another way to salt-water. This is why the Derwent and its tributaries came to give an infusion of cold water into the Ouse, not very far from Goole. And why, each December, as the river spills over its banks, parts of the Derwent valley become a gigantic lake, the haunt of whooper swans and wigeon.

The Moors are at their most beautiful in late summer. Bees which gather nectar from the flowering ling are augmented by domesticated strains. Hives are transported to the moor's edge to take advantage of a great harvest of nectar. Heather honey is so viscid it cannot be extracted from the combs by the usual means and must be cut away.

When grouse are not gorging themselves on bilberries, they shout at each other through purple beaks. The birds, which typify the Moors because of their wild spirit and inability to live anywhere else but on heather, are relative newcomers. After the district had been the playground of glaciers, woodland took over. Then Man appeared, complete with fiery torch and axe, clearing away the trees. In the new open conditions, heather thrived. Eventually it was being managed by landowners for the benefit of sheep and grouse.

Gamekeepers are relatively common. One entered a moorland inn, flopped into a chair near the bar and said: 'We've had all sorts of shooters on t'moors. I thowt I'd got their measure. I called a duke "your Grace". But today we had a bishop. When a rabbit shot up in front of him, I said: "Shoot the little booger, yer Holiness." But I could tell bi t'expression on 'is face I were wrong!'

The West Riding man with a limited vision of moorland magic – as you may recall, he summed it up as 'nowt but scenery' – had been taken at high speed along the Pickering to Whitby route, which runs along the moortops. It's not exactly mountaineering, the highest point being 900 feet above sea level, just beyond the awesome Hole of Horcum which was scooped out by the giant Wade. The traveller follows a road which dips at the Devil's Elbow to pass (or not to pass, depending on the thirst of the driver) the Saltersgate Inn. The peat fire, first lit in 1801, has not been allowed to go out – very often!

Traffic on the Whitby road does not dawdle. There is something intimidating about a road stretching to infinity. The tyres of the cars and lorries positively whine as the drivers give in to their horizon-sickness. Any touroid who eases off on the throttle to look around soon finds that several cars are fidgeting behind, waiting for a moment to pass. It's a lemming-like urge to get to the seaside as soon as possible. One tourist, who later met his tormentor in the main carpark at Whitby, said: 'I didn't know you were in a hurry; you were going at the same speed as me.'

The super-highway passes between the Goathland Moors and Fylingdales, where there was a collection of radomes, the equipment within them giving advance warning (four minutes) of enemy missiles. The radomes were replaced by a stupendous pyramid. Hens at moorland farms learn that they must keep lively with fast traffic about. A daft tale is told of a holiday visitor who saw a hen with three legs scuttering off down a farm track. He followed it and commented to the farmer on the hen's fine turn of speed. The farmer, who said he bred three-legged hens, was asked if these hens were good to eat. He replied: 'I've no idea. I haven't managed to catch one yet!'

Military jets on low-level exercises pass with a whine and a whoosh. The moorland sheep ignore them, though they pass with a sound like a thunderclap. Sir George Cayley, of Brompton Dale, was a pioneer aviator, with ideas fifty years ahead of the Wright brothers. He was just short of a suitable power unit for his aircraft. In 1853, he launched into the air a machine which had all the basic features of what was to become an aircraft apart from that vital engine, but the 1853 venture is regarded as the first man-carrying flight by a heavier-than-air machine. Cayley instructed his coachman to fly the machine. The coachman dutifully took off, landed without mishap, then immediately went over to Sir George and handed in his notice, pointing out that he had been hired to drive, not to fly!

The Moors have their highspots, and none more distinctive in its shape than Roseberry Topping, an outlier of the Cleveland Hills. The Topping falls far short of the required 2,000 ft for mountainhood, but is almost symmetrical and cone-shaped, visible for many miles away across the plain and to anyone following the path along the western rim of the Moors. To the proud folk living round about, this was 't'highest hill in aw Yorksher'. John Speed, the cartographer, mentioned its 'goodly prospecte' and about the middle of the eighteenth century, one of the locals – Thomas

Pierson – put his feelings into verse, beginning:

> Of Atlas mount let poets antique sing,
> Whose summit bare supports the bending sky,
> Of Roseberry's rude rock I deign to write,
> The height of Topping, and its oozing rill.

The oldest rhyme (at least three centuries old) declares:

> When Roseberry Topping wears a cap
> Let Cleveland then beware a clap.

And while in a mood for versifying, it might be the place to mention the clayey nature of the Cleveland plain and to quote a traditional couplet:

> Cleveland in the clay –
> Take two boots, bring one away.

Frank Elgee, whose memorial I had seen near Blakey, was as aware as anyone of the ancient residents of the moor. He also made friends with some families who, not so long ago, were so isolated, living in remote dales, that when a lord, one of a group of sportsmen, saw a mean hovel tucked away in a green pocket, ringed by moorland, he asked: 'How much do you have to pay the poor b— for living there?'

Fifty years ago – nobbut a wink in the Yorkshire story – moorland man was still fairly primitive. He hadn't much brass, so if he couldn't afford a bike, he walked. When a farmer or his man went shepherding, he put a few mutton sandwiches in a pocket of his battered raincoat. One of the Moors farmers used to complain to his wife about not having enough sandwiches, so she cut a whole loaf of bread into two and slipped between them the contents of a corned beef tin. That evening he complained: 'Thoo only gave me one sandwich.'

Today, the moorlander, with his little all-terrain vehicle, can get virtually anywhere without delay. I watched a man ploughing a field in Bilsdale which was so steep he would be able to see little else, when looking forward along the tractor bonnet, than the sky. Tractors came into everyday use during the 1939–45 war. Land-girls learnt how to drive them. They do say that one lass took a defective tractor to the garage and tried to explain what had gone wrong with it. She said: 'I heard a click – just like a shoulder-strap going.' One of the farmers took a new car back to the garage and said: 'It's not rattling reet.'

About the turn of the century, help was secured at the hirings, such as those at Stockton, where the new labourer – and his tin trunk – were conveyed by horse and trap to the moorland farm. The farmer and his wife were soon detailing the duties he would have to perform, for a few pounds a year, plus 'keep'. Eventually, the hired man – tired out as he simply listened to what he was expected to do – said: 'Hey, mister – hast thoo much clay o' t'farm?'

Said the farmer: 'Nay, not so much, but mebbe there's a bit by t'beck. It's reight clarty theer. Why does ta ask?'

The farm-hand said, with a smile curling his face: 'Nay, ah was aimin' ti mak a few bricks i' ma spare tahme.'

Thrift is accountable by the experiences of the past. Sometimes it reaches the point of meanness. One summer's morning, a moorland farmer who was noted for being mean hitched his horse to the mower and, in the meadow, set the blade of the machine as low as possible. He wanted to get the maximum amount of grass. The field was bumpy. The prongs caught in the ground. The shaft of the mowing machine broke. A neighbouring farmer remarked: 'That's what comes o' trying to plew as well as moo.'

Horizons are low. The sky is big. A Cleveland lad who had difficulty in painting some clouds during an art lesson at school was helped out by the teacher, who included some white fluffy clouds. He protested, saying: 'Miss – where I come from, t'clouds is mucky.' The best way to get to know the Moors is on foot, though keep to a footpath – or, at least, to t'ling. Those beautiful Moors can be treacherous.

Old-time pedestrians included Romans using a high-tec road across the edge of Wheeldale Moor, six hundred feet above sea level. The route became smothered in peat and heather. It was rediscovered in 1914. Then the moorland imagination got to work. It was known as Wade's Causeway, after the Friendly Neighbour-hood Giant who, as noted, carried out a major excavation at the Hole of Horcum. Wade and his wife Bel were said to have lived at Mulgrave Castle and she (poor lass) had to trudge twenty miles to Pickering to milk the cows. She needed a good track. Bel collected stones in her apron and Wade positioned them. Or so they say …

The moorland folk are not averse to hard physical toil. Many a farmer got on by scratting (working hard). As recently as the 1920s, an out-of-work ironstone miner came across a small, empty farm which stood almost a mile from the nearest neighbour. The estate agent let him move into it with his wife, two kids and a few 'bits of sticks'. Fifteen years later, the ex-miner had the place in good condition. His favourite word was 'scrat'. Knocking that farm into shape had been a scrat and 'we ain't done scrattin'! When we came, we had a pig and a hen or two. So we scratted till we'd scratted a coo, and that's how we've done it.' His motto was: 'If you want owt, scrat for it; and if you scrat hard enough, you'll get it!'

Ask a Bilsdale man about the weather and he'll tell you straight: 'There's nobbut two soorts o'weather – good and bad.' On a fine day, 'We can do wi' this an' better.' On a bad day, 'It'll get worse afore it gits better.' Ask him how his tatties are developing, and they 'cad do wi' some rain'. On the same day, his hay 'wants some yat sun on it, and then it's not as good as last year's crop'. Sometimes, the weather shrieks. Two farmers, recalling a recent gale, enquired of each other what damage it had caused. One of them didn't know, explaining dolefully: 'It's barn roof. I haven't found it yet.'

In the old days, a moorland family had many mouths to feed. A farmer told a friend at the market that his youngest child had just left school and found a job. The reply was: 'It must be grand to have another pullet laying.' When the lass was about to get married, the two friends met again, and the friend said to the family man: 'I hear tell thoo's gettin' selt [sold] up o' Saturday.'

The moorland farmer, like his brethren throughout the white rose county, doesn't like parting with his hard-earned brass. For the wedding breakfast, the farmer haggled with a hotelier until he was almost giving the meal away and then said: 'How much would it be if I browt mi own ham?'

When another Moors farmer died and in due course his will was published, two old chaps discussed it when they met at Helmsley on market day. The first said: 'He left £50,000.'

Said the other: 'He didn't leave it. He had it takken away from him!'

John Castillo, a Moors dialect writer, wrote a piece to the memory of a local doctor. Castillo noted: 'If I had been as bold as he, I might have wrote down Dr Slee':

Here lies a man, who long has tried,
With mixtures, pills and powders,
To prolong breath and ward off death –
Both from himself and others.

Some said, he much increased his wealth,
With harsh and hard proceeding;
Though many he restored to health,
With blistering and bleeding.

But death, with his old fashion'd dart,
He came one Sunday morning,
And touch'd a tainted tender part,
And laid the Doctor groaning.

Not all the medicine he possessed,
Could heal what then was broke;
And thus the doctor found at last
That dying was – no joke.

Death is not the end of the moorland experience. Living their quiet, remote lives, the folk of the hinterland, flanked by moors, were steeped in superstition and fantasy, believing in such supernatural beings as witches, gabby-ratches (possibly based on the nightjar or goat-sucker) and 'hobs'. While walking along the trackbed which is all that remains of the Rosedale iron-stone railway, I heard a curious sound – a huffing and chuffing, caused by noisy breathing.

Was it the call of a creature from the Jurassic past, mysteriously liberated from a subterranean retreat where it had dozed for a few million years? In this case there was a rational explanation. The sound was caused by three men, linked together by scarves and playing at trains. They hurriedly explained they were on Mr Wainwright's *Coast to Coast Walk* and that Wainwright had said it was in order, on this section of the route, to 'play trains'.

The North York Moors sub-species of hob became attached to a particular family. It was a matter of chance whether a farmer had a good hob billeted with him, and could rely on some help to cure an ailing animal, or he had to tolerate a bad hob, which was nowt but trouble. When I chatted with the veteran walker-author John Hillaby in his moor-edge cottage in Rosedale, there was an inexplicable sound in the otherwise quiet house. John, well-versed in moorland lore, quietly remarked: 'It's only the hob ...'

A Farndale farmer found his hob was so much of a nuisance, he decided to quit his farm for another. So he loaded a cart with his belongings and set off to the new home. Meeting a neighbour, he was asked: 'What's thoo doin', lad. Flittin'?'

From the churn came the voice of the hob – 'Aye, lad, we're flittin'.' The farmer, realising he could not escape his tormentor, shrugged his shoulders, turned round the horse and cart and returned to the old farm.

My old friend Bill Cowley, who after service in India settled down on a Cleveland farm and in his spare time indulged a love for hill walking, devised a walk with the curious name of 'Lyke Wake'. This was mentioned in an old dirge, lyke being a corpse and wake the period of watchfulness before burial. The Cleveland notion was that after death the soul journeyed over the Moors.

In 1955, in a series of articles for *The Dalesman*, which I had the pleasure of sub-editing, he pondered on the possibility of a forty-mile walk across the Moors, between Osmotherly and Ravenscar. It should be completed in less than twenty-four hours. If a walker went at the right season he would kick up heather pollen at almost every footfall – a lovely thought. The Lyke Wake Club soon acquired a character of its own. Bill was the chief dirger. Jean, his wife, was instituted as the chief witch. On the staff were an anxious almoner, harassed archivists, doctors of solefulness and masters of misery. The Lyke Wakers also had a most miserable and melancholy mace-bearer. Social life consisted mainly of wakes. Those who attended wore black or were dressed as an ancient Briton or a druid.

It was Bill Cowley who told me of some pre-war talk in the Buck Inn at Chop Gate. The topic swung to the wonders of plastic surgery. Old Fred Garbutt joined in. 'Oor vet's as good as onny on 'em,' he said ruminatively. 'Last harvest, t'lad chanced ti tek a greeat piece oot ov his thigh wi' t'reaper. He was in a bad way, but t'vet com up tiv a new-cauven [calved] coo, an' he fettled t'lad as well – he just took a slice off t'coo's udder an' stitched it on, shairp as owt. T'lad mended quick, an' noo he's givin' three gallon a milk a day, sucklin' tweea calves, an' doin' a day's work inti t'bargain.'

The popularity of the Lyke Wake Walk led to some linear erosion of the landscape. Alternative routes have been recommended. Some of the footpaths indicated by hatched green

lines on the Ordnance Survey maps are durable and well-cared-for,
an instance being that which extends along the wild undulations of
the moors from near Osmotherley, northwards to the Wainstones.
For miles, the route has been reinforced by great slabs of stone,
much of it from Bolton, Lancs, which were lowered in slings by
helicopter and set in place by dedicated workmen who usually do
the high stretches in summer and then attend to the lowland paths in
winter.

The Cleveland Way (93 miles) is gloriously varied, moorland
stretches alternating with well-wooded dales where, in spring, there
is the azure of massed bluebells and the songs of countless willow
warblers. The White Rose Walk, between Roseberry Topping and
the White Horse of Kilburn, offers extensive views. The North
York Moors Crosses Walk has the novelty of visiting thirteen stone
crosses in a 54-mile journey which begins and ends at Goathland.
Some walkers asked a moorland farmer the way to the next village.
He pointed out a path across a field, said there was a stile, then a
wood, then another stile and ... 'ask again, lads. I've been no
farther than that missen'.

The moorland villages, roofed with red pantiles and with houses
and farms looking at each other over acres of sheep-cropped grass,
are a delight, and especially Hutton-le-Hole, where I enjoyed
visiting R.W. Crosland, a gentle Quaker with an encyclopaedic
knowledge of the Moors. He lived with his unmarried sisters in a
house flavoured by bunches of herbs. Once, slithering into the
village from the moor on snow which had a crust of ice, I shared the
fireside and listened to moorland tales which came with a satisfying
regularity.

He told me of the lad who, in about 1690, visited a Quaker farmer
at an isolated moorland house. The lad did not return. A search and
inquiry failed to trace him. Had he wandered into a bog? Then the
farmer came under suspicion of murder. Years later, the story had a
happy ending. The lad had turned Quaker and did not want to tell
his family. So he surreptitiously emigrated to the new colony of
Pennsylvania, where he married and settled down.

Another moorland story-teller was Major J. Fairfax-
Blakeborough, who lived at Low House, Westerdale, reet at the top
of the Esk Valley. A friend once described his house as being
'twenty miles from anywhere on a wolf-infested moor'. Over forty
years ago, I took advantage of a moonlit (and, happily, wolfless)
night to walk from Castleton to Low House.

When he was not typing, Fairfax-B. would be jotting down impressions and quotations, using a quill pen. He said:

I'm old enough to remember when people believed in witchcraft and fairies. Old men like Bobby Dowson and Nicholas Spink, who ran the Hunt, had tales to tell of a local witch called Peg Humphrey. She frequently led them on bootyless chases, having taken on the form of hare or black fox. When a hound grabbed a leg as she masqueraded as a hare, Peg was lame for weeks after. She put a curse on the dale's farmer who kept the offending hound.' Said Fairfax-B. sadly: 'I don't suppose you'll find anyone now who takes 'em seriously.'

He remembered when those who lived among the hills were unconcerned about 'what o'clock it is', as an old Bilsdale woman put it. When the pointers of her grandfather clock were at twenty to seven, and it struck fourteen times, she knew it was about 5 a.m. and time to get up.

He wrote screeds in dialect, most of his stories centring on a character called Lizzie Leckonby. In one instalment, Lizzie replenished her jam cupboard by a ruse. She developed a bad cold and, 'doctoring hersen with blackcurrant syrup, an' that', she 'telled ivverybody what called that if she nobbut had some blackcurrant, or elderberry, or honey, she could soon backen her cawd an' cough ... Fosst yan, than another, landed up wi' pots o' jam an' jars o' honey ... so Lizzie's getten her jam cupboard filled up again – for nowt.'

A farmer and his family might not have had much money but they ate reasonably well. Fairfax-B. told me of the farmer's son who, visiting a relative in town, sat down for a meal and eyed a sideplate. Auntie remarked: 'Don't you have any plates back on the farm.'

He replied: 'Aye – but not wi' nowt on!'

There is a social life on the North York Moors. At inns like the Lion at Blakey, they used to play tricks on market-fresh farmers who stopped for a drink, leaving their horses and carts outside. One horse was so accustomed to stopping at a wayside hostelry that the driver had to go through the routine of dismounting and entering the pub each time. Another farmer had his horse taken out of the shafts. He reeled out of the inn, stood for a few moments to focus his eyes, and remarked: 'If my name's Jack, I've lost a horse. If my name isn't Jack, I've fun [found] a cart.'

Quite apart from the grandeur of Rievaulx Abbey or Mount Grace, reminding us of past glories, there are little Anglican churches, some with steeples. The best-known moorland parson was Canon J.C. Atkinson, of Danby, an off-comer (Essex) who wrote about local life in his book *Forty Years in a Moorland Parish*. On his first visit, he found stale crumbs on the altar and was told the Sunday school teachers 'must get their meat somewhere'.

A visiting aristocrat, who entered a tiny church, said: 'It's no bigger than my dining-room.'

The vicar remarked: 'And, my lord, the living is not half as good.' In recent times, a new High Church parson proved too much for a rheumatiky farmer, doyen of a country congregation, who said: 'He has us bobbing up and down like a lot of tappets.' There's a strong and simple faith. A man who overheard a couple arguing about religion brought the argument to an end with the simplistic comment: 'If t'prayer books reight – it's reight. If not, clap it at back o' t'fire.'

Methodist chapels give the impression they were designed like boxes, with a porch stuck on the front, almost as an afterthought. A 'wayside pulpit' conveyed, in large letters, some Christian notion. One week, there was but a single word – Think – after which a local wit added: 'Or thwim.' A chapel choirmaster, unimpressed by the effort being put into an anthem, rebuked them with the words: 'Yer stand theer like a lot o' paraffin lamps wit'leets out.'

Cricket was taken very seriously up in thinly populated Westerdale, where two teams were fielded. A visitor asked the skipper of one team who had been picked for a forthcoming game against Sleights. He replied: 'It all depends who turns up.' Also taken seriously, in the Egton Bridge area of Eskdale, is the growing of goosegogs [gooseberries], the subject of an annual show when a winner can be decided by featherweight.

At Grosmont, in the Esk Valley, is Moorsrail, a name given to the North York Moors Railway (to Pickering) which is a preserved and well-run line with about 300,000 passenger journeys annually. Fifty years ago, using the old service from Pickering through to Whitby, I heard the story of a Scotsman and Yorkshireman who, during a rail journey, were bragging about their respective parts of

Britain. On this occasion, the Yorkshireman lost out. He said to the Scot: 'Tell me summat tha can't do – and I'll do it.'

The reply was: 'I canna pay ma fare.'

8 Yorkshire Wolds

As straight as a yard o' pump watter.
[Old Yorkshire simile.]

It is the BIG country. With a BIG sky. A Wolds farmer works on a scale which would leave a dalesman, with his fifty acres of good grassland, gaping with astonishment. An Oklahoman would feel at home here, where a summer breeze rustles miles of corn standing 'as high as an elephant's eye'. At least one Wolds farmer has invested in a light aircraft.

The Wolds are best seen by the traveller on foot, using the Wolds Way or, better still, from the Minster Way of 51 miles, between the Minsters of York and Beverley. A textile man who visited Beverley Minster stared with drooping lower jaw at the vast enclosed space and said to a friend: 'How many looms does ta think they could get in here?'

An awesome sight on the Wolds in late summer is that of thousands of round bales of straw, forming a pattern across the yellow stubbles under an azure sky. Sowing, reaping and threshing have been local obsessions for centuries. When a well-to-do Wolds farmer died, his widow decided to carry on with the aid of the oldest farmhand who, at threshing time, asked: 'What about sex?' She was on the point of firing him when he added: 'We'll need some more secks to put t'corn in.'

The Wolds are formed of a crescent of chalk extending from the Humber to a seaward termination in white cliffs just north of Bridlington. Early Man found the soils on the Wolds easily worked. Norman Billy, fresh from his triumph at Hastings, peevishly 'harried' the North and left large tracts blighted.

105

Archaeologists at the site of the medieval village of Wharram Percy found evidence of prosperous days, checked for a time by the Black Death. A corn-growing community changed to sheep-rearing when the price of wool made it irresistible.

Said a 'Waudsman' who was temporarily down on his luck: 'It's aboot time things picked up. One door closes – and another door slams to!' In the Wolds area, the old social fabric endures. There's a stability about local life. A farm labourer who had worked for an important landowner for fifty years was approached by the agent about the possibility of retirement. The old man replied: 'Nay – I wouldn't have stayed in this job if I hadn't thowt it was permanent.'

As in Devon, another sequestered area, every turn of the road brings another memorable picture – of an old hall, snug behind mossy walls of a village of a few houses, plus a pond in a huge saucer smeared with clay; of farm and shelter-belt of trees, and fields littered with bits of chalk, each so bright it might have its own inner source of light. Yet the Wolds must be the most under-photographed part of Yorkshire.

My old friend Charlie Emett, of Darlington, who has written a walker's guide to the Wolds, summed up typical scenery most picturesquely as 'neat fields of bronzing barley, pale green wheat and darker pigmented peas, all sewn together with dark green hedgerows, dappled brown, spread like a pretty patchwork coverlet beneath a pure, cerulean sky'. Luvly! Charlie, who loves to sniff out an unusual aspect of the rural scene, found, at the approach to South Cave, what he claimed to be the best cucumber-growing area in Britain. 'The straight cucumbers are first class quality. Those which curve slightly are seconds. And those that are almost horseshoe-shaped end up being canned with fifty-six other varieties.'

The Wolds landscape may appear to be Oklahoman in character – one vast tract of land, with the wind drawing a comb through corn or barley – but there are many places where nature is untrammelled. This chalk landscape has a rich variety of flowers. They thrive in old chalk pits, beside village ponds or as linear and unofficial nature reserves where, until recent times, the Wolds had its own railway system. Orchids of various kinds, harebells, cowslips, and a host more, have their flowering seasons under a huge sky.

Butterflies look especially attractive in an area where the tones are light. When I pointed to a Red Admiral, a Wolds friend with a sense of the ridiculous remarked: 'I suppose the next thing to look for is a Three-star General.' The native wit triumphs. Near Beverley, where a signpost bears the legend 'Hutton 1', a cricket fanatic added: 'Not oot'.

This is not 'gee whiz' country in the sense of scenic splendour. The average wold breaks the five hundred feet contour and the highest point, at 807 feet, is not on some remote chalk summit but at the top of Garrowby Hill, which takes the main road from York. From Brantingham Wold, when the clouds have lifted, you might see the cooling towers of Drax power station, standing smooth and white, like huge milk bottles on the doorstep of the Pennines.

Driffield, at the heart of the Wolds, is the traditional market place for dozens of Wolds villages. It thrived with a canal system and with the coming of the railway. It is equally blessed today, being at the junction of four good roads. Driffield Beck is a famous trout preserve. Tykes from the West Riding, who spread out over Yorkshire looking for good 'watter' in which to fish, often came across 'No Fishing' signs.

Two lads from Bradford, who would normally have ignored such a sign, decided instead to walk up to the big house and get permission to fish. The valet who answered the door went off to make some enquiries. When he returned, he said: 'His Lordship acquiesces'.

Said one of the Bradfordians: 'Aw reight then! We'll go somewhere else!'

The Wolds have villages with lovely names – Wetwang, Thixendale, Cowlam, Huggate, Tibthorpe, Duggleby and Wharram-le-Street. Fridaythorpe, though situated above the 500 feet contour, has a lowland look in its duck-haunted ponds. There's Norman zig-zag work in the church. At South Cave, strangers look for a yawning hole in a cliff. Hereabouts, Cave means 'swift stream'. South Cave has its Love Lane (surely a courters' route).

It would be much safer than the field path followed by one Yorkshire couple who soon heard the pounding of hooves and saw a large bull bearing down on them. The young man ran to the nearest hedge and scrambled over it. His lady-love followed, some feet behind, and just managed to emulate him and escape from the bull. When they recovered their breath, she said: 'You'd just been telling me you'd face death for me.'

He replied: 'Yon bull wasn't dead.'

There's a Wolds type of person – and a Wolds outlook. A man who had a tea-cup only half full was heard to say: 'What a lartle sup. I'd nobbut fill a sparrow-neb!' Irene Meggison tells of the irate mother of a tribe of scallywags who used pretty strong language to control her brood and was later heard saying: 'Eeeh, I dean't know 'oo taught t'lartle buggers ti swear!'

H.L. Gee, relating a tale heard in Holderness when times were grim, reported a granny as saying, when she was asked about her health: 'Why, Ah's just middlin' misen, bud mi son, Jim, he's iv a sad way. He's lost two pigs an' two childer. He taks on aboot t'childer, but Ah says tiv him, nivver heed aboot 'em – they're a great deal better off 'an ivver tho cud make 'em; bud Ah is sorry aboot t'pigs. Jim scratted ti get 'em up, an' they wor worth two pund apiece, an' noo they've beeath on 'em died.'

The area was open sheep-walk up to the time of the Napoleonic Wars. There were also lots of rabbits, many of them in warrens which provided fresh meat for the local folk. A poacher, trying to impress a friend with the rural bounty, said: 'When I go rabbiting, I've to lift a couple o' rabbits oot of a burrow afore I can get t'ferret in!' Tidy-minded folk with means, such as Sir Christopher Sykes of Sledmere, frustrated in their farming ambitions by commonland, benefited hugely from the enclosures, which in this region were large and square. The Sykes family created what we now take to be typical Wolds features. New farms were built. Horseshoe-shaped belts of mixed hardwood trees provided bield (shelter) and also yielded useful timber when mature.

The Wolds farms needed a small army of helpers, who were well-disciplined. They expected to work hard. Unwilling men were soon put in their place. A farmer roused one of them on Monday morning with the words: 'It's half past five. Tomorrow's Tuesday. The day after is Wednesday. Half the week gone. And nowt done!'

Florence Hopper told me the story of an old farmer who, in the days when a pound was considered a farm-worker's pay for a week, engaged extra hands to do the stacking. Late in the afternoon, as the men were looking forward to their pay, the farmer arrived in the 'staggarth' and, to the disappointment of the spare hands, offered them 3s.6d. for their day's work. One and all, they refused. One man had nothing to say, so the old farmer approached him, saying: 'Thoo'll tak 3s.6d. if ah offer it to tha, wean't the, mister?' The man said he would be delighted. He took the money. Said the old farmer to the other men: 'Noo, see there, yon fellow's not aboon takkin 3s.6d.' He was met with a guffaw of laughter.

Said one of the workers: 'We dean't wonder. He's a chap from t'village. He's only lookin' on.'

In the lean years of the 1930s, when prices slumped, much of the experienced labour had to be laid off. Crops were meagre. The big country greened up in springtime and was golden with corn in late summer, but this season also brought a splash of scarlet from massed poppies, which were attractive but classified in the farming context as weeds. The 1939–45 war saw immense changes. New types of multi-furrow ploughs bit deeply into the ground. Selective sprays checked the growth of charlock and poppies. Combine harvesters lumbered across the landscape.

The Wolds assumed their tidy state – at a cost. A March breeze lifts dust into the air and gives the impression that the landscape is smoking. An aged family, looking towards the edge of a dust-cloud, see a piece of blue sky and remark: 'There's a piece 'at slipped 'em!' For some years, when there was a fashion for burning the stubbles, walls of fire advanced across the landscape, cooking the worms, scorching the few remaining hedges and leaving an area which for a time looked desolate.

The big country greens up with the springtime and is golden with corn in late summer. Mechanisation, in the shape of the multi-furrow plough, the wide drill and the combine harvester, coupled with ways of controlling the growth of weeds, have transformed the Wolds. The corn grows on the high ground, which overlies chalk or limestone. The farm stock is to be found mainly in the narrow, dry valleys, which keep their greenness even during a week or two of drought.

Almost all the valleys are dry, an exception being that down which the Driffield Beck flows. Here is superb trout fishing. The rights to catch trout are zealously preserved, though a visitor asked a local: 'Will it be a crime if I catch any fish?'

He was told: 'No – it'd be a ruddy miracle.' Large-scale farm operations on the Wolds include the fattening of cattle and sheep and the rearing of pigs and turkeys.

The horse has been greatly revered by the Wolds families, though they have invested heavily in mechanical h.p. On a foggy morning, a horse which is not in the mood for work can easily lose itself in a dale. One of the first requirements of a farm-hand was that he could ride. J. Digby Cooke, a Woldsman I used to meet at best-kept village competition meetings in York, told me of the lad who was given a lively horse, which bucked and jumped in an effort to dislodge him from the saddle. He hung on to the horse for several moments. Then, looking down, he saw the animal had a hind leg fast in the stirrup. He shouted to the horse: 'Hod on a minute. If thoo's gettin' on – I'se gettin' off!'

Horses served the Wolds well. So big were the fields that the men who worked with them slung their bait (food) bags on the horses' hames. It would be 'llowance time before the horse and implement reached the other end of the field. The Wolds wagoners had their period of glory in the first world war. In 1914 they were transformed into an Army unit.

Eventually the number of blacksmiths' shops declined as mechanisation took over. A young town lad who had been a fitter-mechanic settled in a Wolds village where a blacksmith still practised and was asked if he could shoe a horse. The lad was willing to try. The smith left him to it for an hour, having an urgent job elsewhere. When he returned, the horse was lying on its back with all four feet in the air. Yet each foot had been shod immaculately. The blacksmith remarked: 'Yon 'oss doesn't look so good.' The mechanic-cum-blacksmith said he had been worrying about its condition, adding: 'It's looked like that since I took it out of the vice.'

In the Second World War, apart from the bomber stations, the Army held large-scale manoevres twixt Driffield and Sledmere, which was said to be similar to what would be encountered when Normandy was invaded. Tanks moved indiscriminately across standing crops, hedges, fences and (in the memory of one trooper) a lovingly cultivated field of carrots. The free French were camping at Fimber. A solitary bomb dropped at Huggate. Everyone wondered why.

The railway linking Driffield and Malton, long since lifted up, was served by a train known to some as the Malton Dodger and to others as the Driffield Creeper. The line's mile-long tunnel had no railway traffic through it on Sunday. It was, instead, the resort of courting couples. There is also a story of a York man who made his first rail trip, decided that such travel was over-rated, and resolved to cheat the railway company. He would walk home!

I have so far dealt with the more attractive aspects of the Yorkshire Wolds. This area, so close to the North Sea, is noted for the piercing winds which oversweep it. When snowflakes fill the air, Wolds councils spread salt on the roads to keep the remoter folk in contact with the world, though the old people tell stories of farms being isolated by snow drifts for up to six weeks at a time. Years ago, roads were cleared by men with spades. It is said that a man who applied for work at the council offices was offered a spell snow-clearing. He was not keen and remarked: 'What! In this weather?'

The Wolds cannot be fully appreciated from the few main roads. There are dozens of little dales, like deep fingermarks on the low, rolling landscape. These little-known valleys have straightforward names. In the North, and close to the village of Forton, which itself is obscure, are Cotton Dale, North Dale, West Dale, Camp Dale, Cans Dale, Lang Dale and Fleming Dale. The underlying chalk is apparent in a spread of small white stones across the spring landscape. Each stone gleams as though it had its own source of light. Chalk pits, which were opened out to provide stone for building or track-making, are now the resort of rare and lovely flowers.

One feature of the Wolds which is here one day, and gone the next, is the mysterious watercourse, called the Gypsey Race. It flows from Wharram-le-Street through the Wolds to empty itself in Bridlington Harbour.

> The Gypsey I trow is my ancient name,
> My Sponsors Northmen like gold,
> Oh, it's a name of most eerie fame,
> I'm the woe waters of the Wold.

In summer, the Gypsey Race (a name derived, possibly, from the Norse term gypa, or gushing stream) is a mere trickle, but after winter storms and when the snow begins to melt it is a torrent inclined to leave its ancient bed and flow through some of the houses on its banks. The race – or 'woe waters', after its supposed ability to foretell national disasters – was flowing just before the Great Plague broke out in England in 1665. And when the race was a torrent in 1795, a meteor came to earth at Wold Newton. In places, the stream goes to earth, to reappear in the form of springs.

In the chalk landscape of the Wolds, water (or the absence of it) still causes concern. In a drought year, 1826, men from two villages came to blows. The pond at hilly Fridaythorpe, west of Driffield, dried up and, as was customary, the villagers trooped two miles down the hill with their horse-drawn water barrels to take water from the pond at Fimber. When this supply was seriously depleted, Fimber prohibited Fridaythorpe from using the supply. A battle ensued, the weapons being sticks and stones. The intruders from Fridaythorpe, some of them nursing wounds, were beaten back. The Battle of Fimber is still excitedly talked about whenever there is a dry summer on the Wolds.

From the highest farm, Cot Nab, straddling the 800-foot contour on the south side of the York to Driffield road at the top of Garrowby Hill, are clear-weather views right across the Vale of York. The smudge on the horizon is an outlying part of the Pennines.

9   The Pennine Dales

*Noo, awl t'taxgitherers an' knockaboots crooded
roond ta hear Him, an' t'Pharasees an' t'lawyers
chuntered an' said, 'This feller tek's up wi'
good-fer-nowts an' eyts wi' em.'*
[Kit Calvert, of Hawes (translating from St Luke's
Gospel, chapter 15).]

In June 1995 history was made at the Tan Hill Inn which, at an
elevation of 1,732 ft, is the highest pub in England, approached
(with effort) from the head of Swaledale. Ian Cooper and his bride
Carolyne Richardson became the first couple in Britain to marry in
a public house. Sixty folk packed into the stonewalled dining-room
for the civic ceremony.

A crush like that is usually experienced when Tan Hill Sheep
Show is held in spring. Years ago, someone added to the fun by
releasing a Swaledale tup into the inn. The spirit of Susan
Peacock, daleswoman extraordinary, still broods over Tan Hill
Inn, which viewed from higher hills, such as those above
Mallerstang, is merely a white blob against the dun-coloured
Pennines.

Susan, who ran the place in the 1930s, and hardly ever left her
home, was once asked if she went to church or chapel. She replied:
'No, I doesn't – but I respect those 'at does.' In 1935, when the
wireless was a novelty, the BBC made a star of Susan by coaxing
her and the Swaledale Singers down to what she was to describe as
'a bonny big studio' in Leeds. Though 'a shade nervous' at first,
she was soon put at her ease. Asked about her views on
programmes, Susan told the listening thousands: 'A few people

bring the wireless up to Tan Hill with 'em in their cars. I've soon had enuff of it and Michael (her husband) is not struck on it either.'

Halliwell Sutcliffe, an author who spent his best years at Linton-in-Wharfedale, referred to the fell-country of the Pennine Dales as being 'where the lean lands rake the sky'. In the expressive language of the dalesfolk themselves it's the land lying 'on t'tops'. North of the broad grey face of Malham Cove, the countryside has a hard appearance, with cloud-bonneted peaks at over 2,000 feet.

The wind brushes miles of heather and *Nardus stricta* (that tussocky stuff which trips up the walker). Wind also torments the few old thorn trees which cling on to life in unfavourable conditions. The silence is broken by the honk of a carrion crow or crowing of a tetchy cock grouse, which is so much a part of the Dales they named a pub after it – the Moorcock. The bird shouts kowa, kowa, which sounds like 'go back, go back'. A would-be emigrant dalesman, during lean days at the lead mines, set off from his native area but had gone only two or three miles when dawn came. The cock grouse began to call 'go back'. The dalesman, overcome with homesickness, took heed of the bird and returned to his old home.

A man would have to be 'wrang in 'is 'eeard' to live on t'tops, but the ground is well used – picked over by sheep, cropped by beef cattle and, where some heather remains, tended by gamekeepers and used for recreation by battalions of walkers. It is also overlaid by a futuristic pattern of drystone walls. (The latest estimate puts the number of miles of wall in Yorkshire at 48,000, compared with 70,000 miles in England as a whole.)

A Dales wall is really two walls in one, tapering with height, each side bound to the other by large stones called 'throughs' and finished with a row of capstones to turn the weather and make it look tidy. Building a wall is a craft and also an art. The waller does not pick up the same stone twice. A Malham waller said: 'Every cobble has its face, but it isn't any fooil can find it.'

The largest outcrop of limestone in Britain obtrudes in the southern part of the Yorkshire Dales National Park. The limestone is honeycombed with shafts and galleries:

> There's Hunt Pot and Hill Pot,
> Jingle Pot and Joggle Pot;
> A cave without a bottom,
> An' another at's deeper still.

The 'deeper still' joke is still made of t'Buttertubs, those curious, fluted, sixty-foot deep shafts beside the pass linking Wensleydale and Swaledale.

Someone wrote a lullaby for a potholer's baby:

> Sleep, little Stalag-mite,
> Mother holds her Stalac-tight,
> Father's off with torch and rope,
> Leaving Mum with you to cope,
> Whilst he through limestone caves will forge,
> 'Tis this that sticks in Mother's gorge.

The folk hero of the high Dales is the fell farmer, not forgetting his dog. Farm life evolved in isolation. A dalehead family prided itself on its independence and self-reliance, holding on to life during the long winter when, years ago, they were cut off by heavy snow.

One dalehead farmer, who thought his youngest son was getting 'soft' turned him out of the house in a blizzard and told him to 'mak' t'best on it'. Then, repenting, he went out into the atrocious conditions, looking for the lad. Eventually, he came across him, making a large snowball. 'What's ta doin', lad?'

'Nay – I thowt I'd mak' a pillow then go to sleep.' The old farmer snorted, turned on his heels and shouted: 'Don't be so soft.'

The dalesfolk permitted themselves to smile when they heard a curlew calling. Spring had returned. As a Wharfedale farmer put it: 'Ah reckon t'back o' winter's brokken when I hear t'curlew shout.' F.W. Moorman loved the 'tops' and gave us a Wharfedale Lullaby, which begins:

> There's a storm brewin' out on Beamsley Beacon,
>   Thunner an' leetnin' round Simon Seat.
> Up amang t'clouds ride prior, priest an' deacon,
>   T'monks hunt ghosts o' red deer to-neet.
>   Whist thee, my fair,
>   Lullaby, Mary;
> Bolton's brown monks wean't harm thee, my sweet.

It's a lovely poem, though a bit on the sweet side to be truly of the Dales. The monks were intruders for a while – and may still haunt the old green lanes ower t'tops, or the old farmsteads which occupy the site of monastic granges. Their presence may also be detected in the Dales themselves – those steep-sided valleys hewn and polished by glacial action, the glaciers following the lines of old watercourses.

A young doctor, returning to Leeds after spending a few days with friends in Upper Wharfedale, saw a line of figures clad in black, cowled robes at the side of the road as daybreak was coming to the valley. He has a quiet certainty that what he saw were Augustinian canons. One of the incumbents of Bolton Abbey, near where the sighting took place, had heard the slap, slap of sandalled feet on the flagstones in the cellar at the Rectory.

The Pennine Dales reek of sheep. Originally, there were the rough old crag sheep. Now there are a few identifiable breeds, such as Swaledale and Dalesbred. At the approach of a blizzard, the farmers attempt to gather them and drive them to sheltered ground. Otherwise they spend most of their time on Halliwell Sutcliffe's 'lean hands'. Farmers are forever rounding up sheep for lambing, dosing, dipping, spaining (separating lambs from ewes) or when there is the threat of a blizzard on the high grazings.

A farmer who was dosing sheep, spooning into each sheeply mouth some preventive medicine, decided to pour some of the liquid from the large tin in which it had been delivered to a handier, small tin he found among the lumber. An American who saw him at work became excited and shot off a large number of photographs, saying 'gee' at regular intervals. The bemused farmer looked at the old can he was using. On it were the words 'Anti-freeze'.

The Dales farmer knows every animal in his flock. When this ability was questioned by a visitor, he said: 'I reckon thou could tell thy wife among two hundred other women.' Of a Swaledale sheep it was written:

> Back like a brigg
> Tail like a lonk,
> Horns like a sickle,
> Eyes like a weasel.

Swaledales originated through selective breeding on and around Tan Hill. The most famous tup (a male sheep) is Rastus the Ram. Its picture, which adorns the National Park signs, is based on the characteristics of a real tup – a handsome creature, with curly horns, black face and white muzzle. I have seen the mounted head of Rambo, a fine Swaledale tup which went missing, presumed killed, during the grim winter weather of 1947. Over forty years later, the farmer's wife was walking with her daughter when, among the sieves (rushes) she found the skeleton of a sheep. The head carried big horns, on one of which were burnt the initials of her husband. It was the missing tup.

When a teacher told the parable of the lost sheep, and asked why the shepherd, with ninety-nine sheep in the fold, went after the one which was lost, a farmer's son remarked: 'Appen it were t'tup.' A flockmaster could not manage without it! A hill farmer is inclined to put the interests of his sheep before those of his wife, saying: 'If owt happened to me, t'wife would cope. But my sheep depend on me.'

Occasionally, there's a legal battle concerning sheep. A farmer who gave a résumé of the argument to a solicitor was told he would have no difficulty in getting redress. He should most certainly take the matter further. The farmer said: 'I don't think I'll bother. You see – I've given t'other chap's side o' t'argument.' I knew a man in West Craven who wintered hoggs (first-year sheep) belonging to a Swaledale farmer. They invariably lived off his neighbour's grass. The West Craven farmer was meticulous in ensuring that when spring arrived every sheep was returned or, if any had died, full details were available to the owner. I saw him loading three hoggs into the back of his new car. The animals had been missed in the count and he was about to make a special trip to their home farm up t'Dales. Said the farmer: 'They should be good 'uns. They came on a Sunday and they're going back o' Good Friday.' He mentioned the government regulations about sheep-dipping – how the dipper had to wear protective clothing to avoid contact with the substances in the dip which might cause ill-health. The farmer added: 'I'd like to know what happens to t'sheep. Nobody seems to give 'em a second thought.'

The lean, taciturn farm folk of the upper Dales were written about by Alf Wight, the vet, who as James Herriot the author commended Dales life through a series of books with stories which were televised and enjoyed by a world-wide audience. To many people, the Yorkshire Dales, and especially Swaledale and Wensleydale, are Herriot Country. Visitors with a love of Herriotshire visit the Wheatsheaf in Carperby, where the real-life vet and his wife spent their honeymoon.

Alf Wight/James Herriot first became aware of the special beauty of the Dales one evening as he motored across t'tops from Wensleydale to Swaledale. When he was on the unfenced moorland road, somewhere near Grinton Lodge (which became a youth hostel) he let the dog out to stretch its legs and looked down the dale, towards Richmond, marvelling at the ice-sculpted valley, with its hanging woods and the bare sheep ridges round about. He had seen no lovelier country anywhere.

This vet worked at a time when updale families lived at subsistence level but remained at their holdings being as 'heafed' (attached by natural bonds) as the moorland sheep. Sheep do not normally stray from their natal areas, where they might be restrained by drystone walls. In truth, a hill sheep can jump almost as well as a horse trained for the Grand National. I watched a sheep run up a wall and knock off a few capstones. It repeated this until it was able to scramble over. Yet a few yards away there was an opening.

A Dales farmer used to walk, with dog at heel. He had a few sandwiches in a pocket of his raincoat. He would be out and about for most of the day. His successor uses an all-terrain vehicle which can touch fifty miles an hour on the road and not much less on a fellside. The dog rides pillion.

It was at Gayle, near Hawes, that I heard what happened when the first thermos flask reached the area. The hoggs which had been wintered in Wharfedale were being brought back over Fleet Moss to the Wensleydale farms. One of the Pratt family had been to Liverpool shopping and returned with a thermos, which had the mysterious power of keeping liquids hot for hours on end. When snow began to fall on Fleet Moss, Mrs Pratt sent her daughter, with food and thermos full of coffee, to where the men were attending to the flocks.

The daughter rode her pony along the fell road. It was white all over, except for a line down the middle which was the course being taken by the long line of sheep. The first man she saw was handed the thermos and he accepted it gratefully. The top was removed and he gulped down the coffee. His reaction was not surprising. The coffee scalded his throat. After that, the canny dalesfolk tested the temperature of any liquid served to them in 'tin bottles'.

When attending to sheep, a farmer does not have to be in a hurry. A Wharfedale man told me that in t'Dales 'We go by t'almanac, not by t'clock. It's all reet pushin' clocks forrards and backards (for summer time), but it doesn't mak much difference up here. We're ruled bi t'weather.' Sometimes, the seasons run together. In Wharfedale, a man remarked: 'They say winter's coming. I don't believe 'em. They said t'same thing about summer.'

The collie dog makes sheep-farming on the fells possible because, with a dog, a man can round up the sheep quickly, as he needs to do at various times, and especially if there is the prospect of a big snowfall. Farmers pay huge sums for the best dogs. An American visiting a Dales farm saw a dog being put through its paces gathering sheep. When it had brought a dozen ewes to the farmer, the dog went off at high speed and vanished from sight. The American asked where it was likely to have gone. Said the farmer: 'Appen it noticed there was a gap in a wall. It must have decided to fettle it up.'

The west wind brings rain; the north-east wind bears snowflakes which clog the daleheads. Big Bill Alderson, of Angram, in Swaledale, once told me: 'It's not so bad if it doesn't snaw in bed. One neet there was such a whizziker. I'd left the window part open. I slept through yon blizzard. When I woke, everything was covered wi' snaw 'cept where I was ligging. My sister came in to rouse me. I told her to leave t'door oppen and I loped straight out of bed into t'passage.'

Dalesfolk are celebrated for their hospitality. It's your stomach 'at 'ods your back up, they say, and a television crew visiting a Dales cottage were greeted by an elderly lady with the words: 'I've just made a meat-and-potato pie for you, in case you're hungry.' When the pie had slithered down three grateful throats, a pudding was served and there was a cup of tea to follow.

A former farm-hand says: 'Don't talk to me about farmhouse cooking. There must have been lots of first-rate jock-shops – but mine were never among 'em ... And I allus was a good trougher.' Farms with a poor reputation for catering became well-known to agricultural workers. 'If tha goes theer, tha'll get nowt to eat,' it was said. Edith Carr's cooking was developed to cater for quite large families in Malhamdale and on Malham Moor and a basic food supply was close at hand. Hens scuttered about the farmyard. The small flock yielded eggs, cock chickens and, eventually, adult birds for the larder. Geese were reared. They were popular Christmas fare before turkey became the vogue.

Each farm had a pig or two, any surplus porkers, aged about eight weeks, being sold off. Those pigs retained for home consumption were reared on blue milk, a by-product of the butter-making process, also pig-meal and bran. There was a fashion for 'cramming' pigs just before they were killed to attain the highest possible weight. One old lady was seen sitting beside a pig, which she had partly reared up against the gable end of the farmhouse so that she could feed it a succession of oatmeal balls. A drop o' milk put a fair shine on their skins.

At a Dales farmhouse, the kitchen range was an iron structure, incorporating an oven and boiler for water. The whole demanded a weekly application of blacklead. It was quite a performance on baking day cleaning the flues with a special rake and goose-wing. The flour bin held ten stone of plain flour. Self-raising flour was kept in a dresser, along with jam, lots of packets of sugar and coconut. Long since, coconut was very popular.

In the homes of chapel folk, grace was said before meals. This mystified a visitor from the town who, when he saw the bent heads, asked: 'What are you talking to your puddings for?' Chapel folk described strong drink as 't'Devil in suspension'. One, who drank some claret by mistake, covered up his embarrassment, when he was asked whether he liked it, by saying: 'Like it? If it cost owt – it were too dear!' Porridge was a staple food at farm and cottage at breakfast-time. In the days when black treacle was a penny a jar, it was spread liberally over the oatmeal porridge. Lumps in the porridge were called 'dog 'eeards'.

Dales food was plain but wholesome – sad cake, fruit cake, rock buns, which were virtually flour and fat, wi' currants in, plus home-baked bread. Occasionally, a meal might include any cracked eggs. The new farm man was asked if he would like a boiled egg for his tea. He replied: 'Ah yance kent [knew] a man who ate two eggs. And he's wick [lively] yet.' On a visit to town, the dalesfolk might indulge in fish and chips. One who had heard of fish and chips but had never sampled any slipped a few chips in his mouth, then said, dejectedly: 'These chips taste like tatties.'

Kit Calvert, of Hawes, a dalesman extraordinary, is remembered as the saviour of the Wensleydale cheese industry when it was beset by financial problems in the 1930s. The old way of making Wensleydale cheese, in farmhouses, was to take the milk warm from the cow directly to the cheese-kettle by back-can. An aunt of Kit's put a few pints of scalding water into the kettle to lift the temperature to eighty-five degrees; then she put in rennet (the 'starter'). She used the afternoon milk for butter-making and made cheese only from the morning milk.

When either blue (skimmed) milk, or a mixture of half-skimmed and half-new milk, were used, the result was whangy-cheese, which was so chewy (tough) it had to be attacked with an axe. It was not fit for anything but cooking – or it was given to the farm-hand.

Hawes Creamery is posher now than when Kit presided over it, taking over a tradition of factory production which began in 1897. The present creamery had the proverbial new lease of life, in the spring of 1992, when Dairy Crest wanted to close it down, transferring production into (let it be whispered) Lancashire. A management buy-out and some imaginative development, including a visitor centre, has turned its fortunes.

Until recently, the Dales families were very parochial. A farmer (on a push-bike, not in a car) might go no further than t'market or t'chapil. He'd married a farmer's daughter – yan of us! 'Once hill-farmer married town girls, they married trouble,' one of them told me. 'Yon lasses knew all about painting their fingernails, but not much about livestock.' This comment was less than fair. Lots of town lasses became first-rate wives on the Dales frontier – the land between the dale and the high fells.

It was the farmer's wife who held a family together in an upland area. Yet some unkind stories were told about her, the unkindest concerning the farmer who, one evening, saw a light moving across his farmyard. One of his hired men, in his best setting-off suit, was going courting. 'Courting?' queried the farmer. 'Ah nivver took a lantern when ah went courtin.' 'Naw,' said the man. 'Ah thowt not when Ah saw t'missus.'

A diminutive farm man who set his eyes on a farmer's daughter at a dance, contrived to have the last waltz with her, which meant he might ask to walk her home. She told him she lived five miles away, which made him all the keener. On the way, he asked for a kiss. His request was granted, but he was so small he could not reach her. So he picked up a milk kit at the side of the road, stood on it and had his kiss. They walked for another mile or so. He asked for another kiss, but she said: 'One time out – one kiss!'

Said the farm man: 'In that case, I'll throw this milk kit away.'

Dancing mixed up the families and led to many weddings. A beefy young farmer, when thanking a buxom lass for joining him in a quickstep said: 'That were grand. I've not sweat so much since I took a prize heifer to Kilnsey Show.'

Old-time families were big – up to ten. 'I knew a woman who had ten kids twice over … Aye, she lost one and so they had another, to keep the number up to ten.' If a farmer lost his wife, he invariably married again. One man who was thought to be 'old enough to knaw better' had a second wedding day. A friend said: 'He always did knaw better, till he met the widow woman. She knew better still!' It was the young farmers' clubs which mixed dalesfolk up to the extent that a lad from one dale would break with tradition – and marry one from the next dale. In Wensleydale, 'yance hill farmers started marrying girls from "away", they married trouble.'

The cattle are kept under cover from November until May, and February is midwinter in the sense that a farmer then needs to have at least half his stock of hay left to be able to sustain his herd till the spring flush of grass has appeared. A farmer who ran out of hay turned his cows on to frost-stiffened fields. A friend said: 'They've nowt to eat.'

Whereupon the farmer replied: 'No, lad – but look what a good view they've getten.'

The fells had their peat-pots, whence came fuel for the winter, the peat being cut in the traditional way, with two turves propping each other up while they dried in the wind and sunshine. They were then built into a conical stack to await collection. In Swaledale, 'you had some big fireplaces, and when you were finished of a night – say, at about five o'clock – you'd bank the fire up with plenty o' peats. You might put a skepful on, and then you had a fire for t'night. You could varry near roast a beeast on it.'

The green roads and sheep-trods are now scarred by the boots of countless walkers. 'Nay, lads,' said a Swaledale farmer to a small party of hikers, 'haven't you got homes?' It may have been this man who directed a walking party by saying: 'Go through yon wood, then cross t'next field to a farm; then ask again. I've not bin any further missen.' Mr Wainwright's *Coast to Coast Walk* runs through Swaledale which, according to a local song:

> From Hollow Hill Cross
> To Stollerston Stile
> The extent of Swaledale
> Is twenty long mile.

The generations verbally snipe at each other, such as when a farmer saw his son 'doing nowt' and told him to brush down the yard. He handed the lad an old brush, whereupon he said: 'We've a better one than that.' The farmer said it was wise to wear out owd things first.

His son handed him the brush and said: 'In that case – thee brush t'ard out.' The Dales farmer, in turn, likes to take a rise out of visitors. He told a rambler who was looking at a large black bird: 'Yon's a craw [crow]. I've a name for each of 'em.' The rambler was amazed. 'Aye,' said the farmer, 'I calls 'em all craws.'

The Dales themselves are like deep fingermarks on the Pennines. Look at a map, and you see how the rivers are fed by numerous runnels and becks which, printed in blue, resemble the veins on the back of a leaf. Each river – Tees, Swale, Ure, Wharfe, Aire, Nidd, Ribble – has its own character. It was related:

> Wharfe is clear, and Aire is lythe,
> Where the Aire drowns one, Wharfe drowns five.

There's no more down-to-earth folk than the daleheaders. Not only have they a dash of Nordic blood in their veins, but they have to contend with grim weather, thin soils and long, long winters. Hannah Hawkswell, who became famous for her solitary life back o' beyond, appeared in a television film called *Too Long a Winter*. She didn't get nostalgic about the 'good old days'. And once she left the farm where she had been raised and outlived other members of her family, she had no inclination to return.

Dalesfolk have a realistic attitude to life. Returning to the chapel theme (and the chapel was at the heart of much of the social life in the upper Dales) I recall preaching in an updale chapel which served a scattered farming community. Almost the entire population within a radius of three miles gathered here on the Sabbath afternoon. On the front pew was the latest baby, in a carry-cot, and sitting in a back pew was the oldest worshipper. He's lived so long that someone mentioned (though not within his hearing): 'I reckon t'Almighty must have forgotten him.' I looked from the pulpit on to the proverbial sea of faces and began a children's address – a somewhat fanciful story. I should have known better. The oldest of the old men rose stiffly to his feet and said: 'We want none o' thee fairy tales here.'

Prayer meetings were the spiritual power houses of t'chapels, though sometimes inter-denominational rivalry came into the prayers. An old chap exclaimed: 'We thank Thee, Lord, that although things is bad wi' us, they're warse off at t'Prims [Primitive

Methodists].' Methodists once had a special awareness of those who had a problem with 'strong drink'. At a North Craven village, a Sunday school teacher repeatedly asked a small boy to tell her when he could write his name. When he proudly reported that he could write, she asked for a demonstration. That wee chap obliged. He had signed the pledge that he would refrain from strong drink. At the Band of Hope they sang:

> Merry Dick you soon would know
> If you lived in Jackson's Row;
> Each day with a smiling face,
> You will see him at his place.

The chorus ran as follows:

> My drink is water bright, water bright,
>   water bright;
> My drink is water bright, from the
>   crystal spring.

If I was 'preaching away', I'd usually get an invitation to tea from one of the flock, but not always. Then I had to 'drop in' somewhere, hoping they were just about to sit down for tea. At one place, the tea was weak – hot water browned off. I like it 'as hot as hell, and black as t'fireback'. The farmer said to his wife: 'Brew another lot, lass. This tea's so weak it wean't waddle out o' t'pot.'

Dales farmers detest bookkeeping. An accountant sighs as he opens an attaché case and sees that it contains a mass of receipted bills and lots of bits of paper on which the client has scribbled. Before the National Health Service was introduced, a farmer had a course of treatment from the doctor and then settled up his account. He started counting out some grubby pound notes. The doctor said he would take a cheque. 'Appen so,' said the farmer, 'but thou's going dahn in my accounts as three loads o' muck.'

An Airedale friend was always bragging about how he had 'diddled' the Inland Revenue. And once, cheekily, he went to the office. When he was asked the nature of his inquiry, he said: 'Nay – I've nowt to ask you. I just thought I'd come and see who I work for.' The old chap who got in a tangle over his tax matters received a visit from an inspector who said, in a kindly fashion: 'I've come to help you fill out your form.' They discussed labour costs. The farmer said he had one labourer who was paid £50 a week and got two weeks holiday, 'and t'half wit, who worked all hours for nowt and got a new pair of fustian breeches at Martinmas.' The inspector said he would like to meet the half-wit. The farmer replied: 'Tha's talkin' to 'im.'

No farmer admitted he was doing well. The best he might say was: nobbut middlin'. He had a lot to moan about, especially the weather, the subject of many an old dialect poem, such as a Yorkshire farmer's lament, which begins:

> Rainin' ageean Ah deea declare;
> It's twaa days wet for yah day fair:
> Warse tahmes than theease was nivver seen,
> Us farmers'll be beggar'd clean.

John Hartley, the West Riding dialect writer, wrote on somewhat similar lines:

> It wur raanin', an' snawin', an' cowd,
> An' th'flagstoans wur covered wi' muck,
> An' th'east wind booath whistled an' howl'd,
> It saanded like nowt but ill luck.

The old isolation broke down with the coming of motor vehicles. T'owd hoss had previously provided the motive power for the upland communities. Those families with horses were able to use them to go to town on market-day. A woman who told a friend she had been riding was asked: 'Horseback?'

She replied: 'Aye, lad – over half an hour ago.' Much fun was reported when market-fresh farmers, with their horses and traps, let the horses direct them homewards.

The Dales bus bridged the gap between horse, Shanks's Pony and private car. The bus carried almost everything, not just people. I travelled on a Pennine bus between Clapham and Skipton when the most vocal of the passengers was a goat. Once, at Settle, a young man carrying a rope ladder entered the bus. An old lady demanded, Yorksher-fashion: 'Are you one o' these potholer chaps?' The young man nodded his head. 'Ay, lad,' said the old lady, 'doesn't tha think tha'll spend enuff time below t'grund wi'out going there now?'

It is related that a frail old lady, who slowly climbed the steps into a bus, anxious not to upset her basket, was given special treatment by the driver, especially when she told him she was going to hospital and would he drive slowly. He did as he was requested and also helped her from the bus at Skipton. She thanked him and added: 'I wanted you to drive carefully because I made a jelly for a friend in hospital. The jelly hadn't quite set when I left home.'

When the time came for the Dales farmer to 'cross Jordan' or 'go to glory' – no one in the Dales actually died – he did not make too much fuss. One man was harassed in his last hours by chapel friends who asked him to remember them to loved ones who had gone before. These were named. The dying man reared himself up and used his last breath to say: 'Does ta think, when I gits to heaven, I'll have nowt better to do than clomp about looking for your Jack and your Fred?'

Typically, a farmer saved his brass in order to impress his friends after his death, for the local newspapers published details of how much had been left. One man, a skinflint bachelor, occasionally permitted himself a smile, and was doubtless thinking of his bank balance. He died. The will was made known. There was just one snag. On the week it should have been mentioned in the newspapers, they were not published. The printers were on strike!

10 Mill Towns

Wheeare t'ducks fly back'ards ter keep
t'muck aht o' the'r een [eyes].
[Said of several old West Riding towns.]

'Nice morning?' I commented to a man in Skipton.

'Aye,' he replied, 'and thou gets thi share on it.' He was one of t'older end, who grew up in the days when we were proud to be associated with the West Riding. He enjoyed life without getting into a lather about it.

Nice mornings were not that common in the days when every mill-town, however small, had its canopy composed of cloud and smoke from mill chimneys. Mill-town women fought an unending war against muck. Woe betide anyone who walked on newly swilled flags! A house-proud lady was in the habit of donkey-stoning the doorstep to outline it in yellow and also blackleading t'tram-lines where they crossed the front of her house.

Mill-towns, occupying the steep-sided valleys of the South Pennines (a name devised by the tourist industry), and spreading across the tops of hills at an elevation approaching a thousand feet (where formerly there were nobbut crows and curlews) used to be mucky and unkempt. A clear demarcation existed where t'town stopped and what they used to call t'countryside began. Now most of the mill chimneys have gone, many a mill has been converted to another use, some chapels have become furniture repositories, and slums have been cleared and converted into car parks, complete with toilets.

People have built bungalows in t'suburbs wherever they could find room for 'em. A woman who used to live in a mean street of terrace houses persuaded her husband to take out a mortgage on a new bungalow. When she had furnished it so that it looked like the window of the Co-op furnishing department, she invited along her old friends, keen to make a good impression. She had already begun to 'talk posh' like her new neighbours. One of the visitors said: 'What about rates?'

The social-climber replied: 'We don't have any rates. Just mice.'

Everything's cleaner than it was. Gardens have never looked better, though roses now pick up black-spot, which they never did when the air was laden with soot. Butterflies revel in the summer warmth where once they got their wings bedraggled. Will Clemence, a West Riding man with a pawky sense of humour, wrote a poem many moons ago about a lad's desire to be a 'butterflea':

> Ah wish't Ah war a butterflea,
>   Wi' gurt big wings 'at flapped;
> Ah'd fly reight aht o' ahr front door,
>   Th' wouldn't hawf be capped!
>
> Ther'd be noa need to climb a wall,
>   Ah'd fly reight ower t'top;
> An' if me wings war warkin',
>   Well, Ah could allus stop.
>
> Ther'd be noa gerrin-up at eight:
>   Yer see – ther'd be noa need.
> Ah s'ouldn't hev to goa t'schooil
>   Cos butterfleas can't read.
>
> Ah'd niver get near t'oven door,
>   Ah'd singe me wings, yer see.
> O' second thowts nah, come to think,
>   Ah'd reyther just be me.

Even t'owd Co-op has changed into a Food Fare, on super-market lines, if it has survived at all. Whatever would we have done wi'out t-Co-op divi? Or the gossip and tales heard while waiting? A Co-op grocer and one of the best friends of the local turf accountant were chatting about a recent race meeting. The grocer said: 'I'm told you picked a slow 'un.'

The customer replied: 'Aye – I should have noticed that t'jockey had takken a suitcase wi' 'im.'

This district has its secrets, one being the location of the Sunday school in the Calder Valley where, on Easter Monday, members of the International Order of the Hen-pecked Club gather for talk, lunch and tea, at rock bottom prices. (The old West Riding teemed with curiously named organisations, one being known as the Greasy Nose Club.) The club has had trouble in getting candidates because few husbands – or perhaps it should be their wives – wanted to be associated with the word 'hen-pecked'. The whole joke of the Order is that no one who is truly hen-pecked would be allowed by their respective hen-pecking wives to join such an organisation.

A member of the Hen-pecked Club, who claimed he actually loved being hen-pecked (and who proudly displayed his certificate of membership in the lounge) told me of the Yorkshireman who died and went to heaven, discovering there were two entry doors – one marked 'Henpecked Husbands' and the other 'Un-henpecked Husbands'. A long queue had formed at the first-named door but there was no one waiting where the notice proclaimed 'Un-henpecked Husbands'. He entered and met St Peter, who asked: 'Why did you choose this door?'

Said the Yorkshireman: 'T'missus told me to.'

In the days when heaven and hell were vivid images for Nonconformist minds, a Keighley man arrived at the doors of heaven, where St Peter asked his place of origin. 'Ah comes from Yorkshire,' said the new arrival.

'Come in,' said St Peter, warmly. He added: 'But don't expect us to make Yorkshire pudding for one.'

They tell of an old reprobate from Halifax who died. Several years later, his daughter 'passed away' and arrived in heaven, where she enquired if her father was there. St Peter tapped some keys on a celestial computer and nodded. 'May I see him?' asked the daughter. St Peter did not think there would be time for this. However, he tapped more keys on his celestial computer and then reported that father was to be found not far away. He would take her to see him. They entered a wonderful room, where the old reprobate was reclining, attended by an attractive woman. Said the daughter: 'Is that his reward?'

'No,' replied St Peter, 'it's her punishment.'

One of the highlights of the mill-town year was the Whitsuntide procession, when hundreds of Christians – men, women and children – walked, with banners flying. Now most of the chapels are full of echoes – if they survive as chapels at all. The days when a preacher could raise the spiritual temperature till there was a chorus of 'Amens' and 'Hallelujahs' are long gone. One preacher, occupying a high pulpit, shouted out his message, waved his hands and twisted his body with religious fervour. A child huddled closer to her mother and asked, nervously: 'What would happen if he got out?'

Sunday is now the busiest day on the local golf course. Mill-town folk, accustomed to complying with the old philosophy that 'the devil has work for idle hands', do not make good golfers. They're too restless. One newcomer to the sport, who didn't like dawdling, hit the ball hard and it fell at the centre of the first green. 'Nah, then – what 'appens now?' he enquired.

His companion said: 'You have to hit the ball into this little hole.'

The mill-town man snorted and said: 'Why didn't ta tell me t'first time?'

Hebden Bridge is a typical mill-town – only a little more so. It could be an Alpine village, wrote a Yorkshire journalist, referring to this compact little place. If there is a Swiss-ness about Hebden Bridge and other industrialised communities on the Pennines, it is that many of the buildings appear to have been stuck on impossible-looking slopes. A motorist travelling between Hebden Bridge and Heptonstall, which breaks the skyline, must first use a 'turning circle' or invest in an elastic-sided car.

The mill-towns of the south-west are, in my opinion, where the real Yorksher spirit endures. There's a homely wash of Yorksher words and expressions which helps to sustain a pride in belonging. Hundreds of refugees from Lancashire have tended to live north of the Aire Gap, in places like Settle and Giggleswick. The mill-town folk had to 'scrat' for a living. They'd been doing it for years, for the word has a Danish origin. They 'scratted' in the handloom period and they scratted when t'mucky mills came and, if they hadn't scratted, they would have had 'hunger knock'.

Now, when t'owd folk are propped up by the State, they still scrat. St Vitus must have been born in t'West Riding. The men are a little more relaxed. When it's sunny and warm enough, a remarkable migration takes place. Elderly men move, with newspaper and pint pot full of tea, from t'fireside to the front doorsteps – to sit, to sip, to read or watch the world go by.

Heritage is big business in many of the mill-towns. The local information centre, run with devastating efficiency by middle-aged women, is now (rather than the parish church) the principal attraction, especially for the children, who have a passion for collecting free leaflets. The information centre has details of everything from geology and vernacular architecture to industry and the special local type of cast-iron drain-covers.

Pride is everywhere evident. Tunnel End, on the Huddersfield Narrow Canal, is (to the information centre assistant) not only one end of a tunnel but a feature of the longest tunnel on the highest section of canal in Great Britain (hurrah!). Information is sometimes dispensed with an amusing tale, such as that of the bargee who was swept overboard by a lively tiller. Embarrassed, he quickly scrambled back on to the barge. When asked if he had got wet, he replied: 'No – I wasn't in long enuff.'

Countryside Rangers in Land Rovers direct people to an area which is austere, ribbed with drystone walls, and with old thorn trees wheezing in the wind. It's served up in brochures with a big dollop of romance. Here and there are modern eyesores – such as windfarms, like something from an H.G. Wells science-fiction story. They do say that all the Pennine windfarms are controlled by a nice little chap sitting behind a console at Hemel Hempstead.

The wind at Haworth 'wuthers' – according to Emily Bronte. An American was telling a Haworth man about the extremes of weather at home. He spoke of violent winds, lightning, thunder, hail and snow. The Haworth man listened patiently to the catalogue of climatic extremes, then said: 'I've known when we had yon lot in twenty minutes.'

Sam Dyson, of Ponden Farm, near Haworth, is one of the great characters of what has become known as 'Brontëland'. I use the word character in the sense of someone who has an individualistic outlook on life. Sam, who has long been a farmer and a sheepdog trialist, is now a little too stiff in the legs for gallivanting about the Moors. His father was a greengrocer who 'hawked' in Great Horton, 't'other side o' Bradford'. He got his greens at Bradford Market, setting off at four o'clock, and (said Sam) he'd have fed a hundred pigs by then.

Sam (like his Dad) spent part of his working life in t'mill – and he hated every moment of it. Sam and his new wife, Peggy, bought Buckley Farm, then moved to Ponden. 'When we got to Buckley, it was chock-a-block wi' sheep. Other people's sheep. Everyone was eating us out of home and harbour. My father said: "Tha'll bank (go bankrupt) here." ' Sam had little idea what to do:

We were hard up – jumping from twig to twig. Them at wanted paying were paid first. We kept t'others waiting a bit.

We had a committee meeting – me and t'missus here – to see if we could afford to buy a dog. We went to Thompsons at Cullingworth and bought a little hairy dog. It cost us five pounds. Thompsons said: 'Whatever you do, don't let it off t'lead for a week or two or it'll come straight back home. We've sold it afore and it allus comes back.'

[Peggy, determined it would not go away, buttered its pads and then left it to lick the butter off.] We let it out, morning after, and it never went nowhere. The fields were full o' sheep, as usual, and that dog ran those sheep. Wherever they went, it was just there in front of 'em. If they went through a gap 'oil or over t'wall, it was waiting for 'em. It was a marvellous dog.

Sam is known far and wide for his sheepdogs. A collie dog is the Artful Dodger of the Moors. 'Sometimes, with t'wind right, you're working it up to three-quarters of a mile away. I've stood at Withens with Old Mac and there's been some sheep that distance away. I've put Mac off on t'top side of Withens – reight round yon 'lotment (allotment) side, and it's got 'em for me.' It depends partly on the weather and partly on the way the dog has been 'brokken in'.

It was a treat to sit with Sam as he turned the pages of a photographic album and commented on the pictures. 'That dog was got by that dog and it was as blind as a bat. It could see nothing. But I got fifty out of fifty at Meltham with it. I put it off and it went right round t'field. I stopped it at twelve o'clock, brought it on to the sheep, so that it could smell where they were, and it went on to get maximum points.'

Sam judged at sheepdog trials held in Northallerton. Two brothers were among the competitors. One was a champion ploughman; he put his dog off and it picked up three sheep – big heavy sheep – and brought them through the first obstacle. 'As they were coming through, one sheep laid down. He left that and went on. He started on his drive and got to a hurdle. Another sheep dropped on t'floor.' Sam considered it was no use judging him any longer but he still went on. 'He got to t'pen. He was trying to pen one sheep. I thought: "I've never sin owt as funny as this in all my life." Anyway, I left him on. When the stewards went round, there were two sheep dead. Two dead sheep! And he tried to pen one!'

A good sheepdog is one 'wi' a bit o' class and enough eye to steady itself on the job. You don't want a dog that is forever flying about ... Size doesn't matter. It depends on what kind of heart it has. The best type is one that'll stand straightening-up (training) and yet when you've finished with it, is still pals with you. If it starts to sulk or owt like that, you don't get nowhere.'

When I got on to the subject of how much a good dog costs, Sam said: 'My job's been making sheepdogs, not buying 'em.' He had bought his first dog for £5 and 'it broke t'bank'. Peggy recalled that the purchaser had given them two shillings back – for luck. It seems that £500 is a common price today but that the best dogs claim well over £1,000. A really good dog is beyond price.

The southern Pennines provide good walking country, especially for those with the time and energy to follow the Pennine Way from Edale, in Derbyshire, to Kirk Yetholm in Scotland. The hilltops are liberally plastered with peat. And if a walker is not 'plodging' through peat, he or she is having ankle-massage from the innumerable tufts of Nardus grass.

To list all the mill-towns and mill-villagers would be to invite writer's cramp. There are dozens of them, ranging from the giants (like Huddersfield and Halifax) to those who spread themselves along a road (like Cowling, locally known as Cowinheeard, between Keighley and Colne). Slaithwaite, locally pronounced Slowit, was t'place 'wheeare they raked t'mooin aht o' t' cut [canal].'

Typical of a host of little mill-towns is Holmfirth, a hillside place where local people develop muscles like Sherpa's from perpetually climbing and descending roads and steps. On to the old mill-town life was grafted the lantern slide industry of James Bamforth, using local folk as models and projecting slides in a sequence with a story-line or to illustrate a popular song of the time. At the time of the 1914–18 war, Bamforths were turning out picture postcards with sentimental themes. The company's fame was based largely on the comic cards which featured fat ladies and anaemic-looking husbands and unruly children in seaside locations, which had a ready sale when the Lancashire coastal resorts were swamped by holidaymakers.

Holmfirth also basks in the glamour of a successful television series, *Last of the Summer Wine*, with goings-on at Sid's Café and Nora Batty's house, up t'steps (two local buildings selected by the BBC for location filming). Higgledy-pickledy Holmforth was traversed, somewhat aimlessly, by the television characters – Compo (who wears wellies and talks incessantly about ferrets and Nora Batty), Foggy (the pretentious one, who has inflated a modest Army career into one of major action) and Clegg (the thoughtful, somewhat shy one, with some amusing 'one-liners') – three types one might see in any community but which, at Holmfirth, draw from the viewer constant titters, with periodic belly-laughs.

Old Haworth has a hillside setting. I used to entertain the idea, such was the steep approach to Brontëland, that if I removed one of the stone setts the rest would come shuttering downhill. Haworth folk stoically endure the fame which sprang from the Brontës and which led to the village becoming the second most popular literary shrine in the land. The Worth Valley Railway, buoyed by favourable publicity – for it is excellently run – is still being visited by thousands who have seen the film version of *The Railway Children*, by E. Nesbitt. Most of the filming was carried out at Oakworth.

At Haworth, and elsewhere, the heritage business whips up sympathy for the poor handloom workers who had their lives shattered by mechanisation, to the extent that when a gormless Nottingham lad called Ned Ludd peevishly broke some machinery he was operating, he was hailed as a hero and prompted the Luddite movement, which specialised in machine-wrecking. The handloom weavers had their own cycle of boom and bust. In the early days of industrialisation, people lived in squalid conditions and were exploited, mechanisation did overall create great prosperity for most and many mill-owners had the welfare of their workers at heart. Among them was Theodore Taylor, of Batley, a pioneer of profit-sharing.

The Rochdale Pioneers get most of the credit for starting the Co-operative Society, but there were other pioneers in Yorkshire where, it is whispered, the new ideas of co-operation were first put forward. The supermarket chain Asda had its beginnings in western Yorkshire. My friend Sam Dyson, sheepdog trialist, has been known to give a shrill whistle when in the supermarket to alert his wife to his presence and position.

Halifax, now best-known for its building society (the world's largest) and Mackintosh's Toffee (the world's tastiest), was once feared by vagrants and wrongdoers because it gave them short shrift – using a gibbet to lop off their heads – hence the lament: 'From Hell, Hull and Halifax, Good Lord deliver us ...'

> At Halifax the law so sharp doth deal,
> That whoso more than thirteen pence doth steal,
> They have a gin that wondrous quick and well,
> Sends thieves all headless into Heaven or Hell.

It was also known for its pretty girls – though the rhymester was unfair on a neighbouring village:

> Halifax is built of wax,
> Heptonstall o' stooan:
> I' Halifax ther's bonny lasses,
> I' Heptonstall ther's nooan.

Wilfred Pickles, a Halifax lad, is still well-remembered as the BBC newsreader because, during the 1939–45 war, when the BBC Home Counties accent ruled, he stuck to his West Riding accent. One night he ended a news bulletin with the standard words, followed by the traditional northern 'Good neet'. One writer had foretold that when Wilfred had his début he would surely say: 'Here is the news and ee bah gum, this is Wilfred Pickles reading it.'

Wilfred later went on to develop his northern comedy in the quiz show *Have a Go*, in which he asked each contestant: 'Are yer courtin'?' and heard one man describe his favourite drink as 'a cup o' tea wi' some senna pods in', the latter being taken by anyone who 'hasn't bin' for a long time.

Halifax glories in its Piece Hall, described as 'a unique piazza-style quadrangle' and built in 1776. It was intended for the sale of pieces of cloth. Halifax has the oldest of the choral societies but perhaps the most famous is that at Huddersfield, where massed voices are raised in pre-Christmas presentations of Handel's *Messiah*, an oratorio which the old West Riding took to its heart.

A satire which appeared in the *Colne Valley Almanack* of 1932 included these priceless observations on t'*Messiah*:

There wor a bit o' bother abaat some sheep 'at wor lost. Ah don't know who they belonged to, but they must ha' been champion twisters and turners judgin' bi t'words an' fancy music. One lot o'singers must ha been very fond o' mutton, because they kept on saying: 'All we like sheep'. Ah couldn't help saying to a chap next to me: 'It's all reight is sheep i'moderation, but gi me a bit o' beef underdone.'

He looked daggers at me and said 'Shush.' So Ah shushed.

This piece of comic writing has a lively ending:

Ah wor feelin' a bit stiff an' a bit stalled, Ah'm baan to confess, when everybody i' t'audience stood up, an' t'band an' singers an' a chap wi' a long trumpet, started t' 'Halleluyah Chorus'. By gum, lad, it wor fair grand. It med mi back go into cold shivers, specially when they said it wor baan to rain for ivver an ivver. Ah'd had mi bob's worth, so Ah pushed me way aat, an' made me way to t'station afore t'train came on, as Ah'd forgotten me umbrella.

Huddersfield is renowned for its town hall, venue for the annual pre-Christmas presentation of the *Messiah*. It is also famous for the length and dignified style of its station façade. The mills of Huddersfield turn out worsted cloth, which is made of 'tops', all the fibres lying parallel to each other in the yarn. Ordinary woollen materials are woven in the same way, having warp and weft, but the yarn is only roughly straightened. 'The fibres lie a bit higgledy-piggledy,' I was told, in non-scientific terms. Huddersfield-made woollens were usually for the better end of the ladies' dress market.

Dewsbury grew with the shoddy trade. This did not mean that local cloth was of poor quality, simply that it was skilfully made from recovered wool, including the waste from other processes, plus the gleanings of the innumerable rag-and-bone men who used to infest the mill-town streets.

Batley, Morley and Dewsbury – mill-towns all – comprised the heavy woollen district because they made these heavier cloths for the cheaper end of the clothing trade. It was at Batley that I heard the tale of a visitor to a terraced house who – when an attractive daughter of the house appeared with a zinc bath and set it before the fire – was embarrassed and said he must leave. Her father said:

'Nay, have another cup of tea.' Shortly afterwards, the daughter returned with a large kettle containing hot water, the first of many that would half-fill the bath. The visitor again said he must leave. 'Nay, thou's welcome to stay,' said Dad. Then the daughter began to undress. The by now greatly embarrassed visitor made for the door. Said Dad: 'Come back. She's a careful lass. She won't splash you!'

My latest sortie into the mill-town part of Yorkshire was a walk along the canal bank from Sowerby Bridge to Hebden Bridge. I was on the borderline between chip country and mashed potato country and also between the black pudding (Lancashire) and Yorkshire pudding. Strangely, after years when only the Yorkshire folk could make real Yorkshire pudding, it is now available from supermarket refrigerators, with or without fillings, a variation on the old theme. This commercialised Yorkshire pudding is quick to cook and good to eat, though it's not quite how Mother used to make it.

Sunday dinner was distinguished by a roast, usually 'a big lump o' beef', which had to be cooked slowly so that it was tender. Yorkshire pudding was made from a mixture prepared a couple of hours before it was needed. 'If you let it stand, it bursts the starch granules,' I was told by one veteran, using a surprising burst of A-level lingo. When the meat was 'just about cooked' (in those days, you went by intuition and good training rather than little knobs and thermometers) you put the roast on a dish in front of the fire, having poured off the browning ready to make some gravy. Into the tin went good beef dripping. The tin was placed in the oven until the fat was so hot it began to smoke.

Now the crucial stage. Just before the Yorkshire pudding mixture was to be poured into the dish, you added a drop of cold water from the tap, beat it up quickly, brought the dripping-tin out of the oven and put the mixture straight in, as quickly as possible. Then it was placed in the hot oven and left for half an hour. The Yorkshire pudding was served as the meal's first course.

For my canalside walk, I had the company of Bob and Colin, two fell-walking friends. It was rather like an episode from *Last of the Summer Wine*. We would converge on Hebden Bridge, where Bob said there should be plenty of parking space. There wasn't. Colin, after touring the suburbs, inched his car into a gap between two vehicles under the amused stare of a local mill-worker. He appeared as Colin began shuffling the car gears. We thought he had emerged from the workshop to give us some help with parking. Instead, he sat on a wall-top, with a smile of amusement on his face and a pint mug of tea in his left hand. He found our efforts entertaining. The Hebden Bridge tea-drinker confirmed that the river, which had the colour of Stephen's blue-black ink, was the Calder. 'There's a dyeworks upstream. And they've bin 'aving a bit o' trouble wi' t'local sewage works. Fish seemed to thrive. But nobody fancies eating 'em.'

We took another car to Sowerby Bridge and walked back along the towpath of the Rochdale canal, part of the trans-Pennine Canal which, opened in 1804, led to a stirring period of industrial development. My love of walking towpaths began in my native mill-town, Skipton, where the Leeds and Liverpool Canal was simply referred to as t'cut and the path as t'cut bank, a resort of geriatric walkers, anglers who occasionally hooked passing barges, and (at night) by amorous cats and courting couples. I heard a good deal of local canal lore. When barges were hauled by horses, one of the animals jumped in the canal every time it reached a certain bridge. It then struggled out again and continued as though nothing had happened.

Bob became nostalgic and told us of a family holiday on a canal barge which they collected at Dewsbury. 'You try telling folks you're going on your holidays from Dewsbury and you'll raise an eyebrow or two.' Between the canal and the Calder was a no-man's land of bracken, bramble and rhododendron, the last-named in full bloom. In the weed-strewn area near the shambles of a lock (soon to be restored) the air was full of flitting, chirruping house martins, some of which were dipping to drink and others engaged in collecting pellets of mud for their nests. The Rochdale Canal appeared to view just behind where a new three hundred yard section of canal would provide a vital link with the canal system of the east. We reached the towpath via the carpark of a local supermarket.

The Rochdale Canal had shrunk to a few pools. Sunshine brought a sparkle to the water and a gleam to discarded supermarket trolleys and a Coke tin. Mills and terraces of luvly West Yorkshire stone flanked the old waterway. We entered our first tunnel and detoured at a closure notice indicating that 'essential maintenance work' was in hand – very essential work, no less than cutting out the canal after years of neglect.

The detour led us across a bridge which was a rainbow arch set in stone. I saw my umpteenth old man, sitting on a doorstep, one of those in Canal View. He was sipping tea from a pint pot, which is almost as good as a vacuum flask for keeping liquids warm. The canal-workers were a well-known civil engineering firm, and the men had the rich speech of Old Oireland. One of them had just met his Waterloo (mobile closet, set down on the canal bank).

The canal, in the water-holding sense, began at the next bridge, and held a summer flush of minute plant life, in appearance not unlike pea soup. The surface was broken by the finger ends – no more – of rubber gloves, lying close together. Should we go to the foreman and demand a re-count of his workers? Instead, we had our first 'butty stop' in an idyllic spot, canopied by trees in summer foliage but lying between the blue-black canal and a large sewage works. Then a duck appeared with half a dozen lively offspring. The birds happily received bits of bread from our sandwiches, though one duckling (gulping down a large piece) appeared to develop a list to starboard. The old duck squawked a warning as a carrion crow passed overhead.

The Rochdale Canal turned out to be a duck factory. Nesting in the reeds which give jungle-like conditions to the banks were a host of birds, some being mallard and others a cross between mallard and Aylesbury (as testified by white patches on the plumage). Large broods were hatched out, only to be thinned out by natural predation, leaving a tough nucleus, unafraid of humans and addicted to sandwiches. Among the satanic mills were tracts of floriferous ground, bright with summer flowers. The purple spires of foxgloves were everywhere. A limited number of the white variety stood out against a tangle of bramble and nettles.

At Luddenden Foot (flatten all the vowels) we saw a housewife shake a tablecloth at the door of her house. The food scraps descended directly to the ducks waiting on the canal to receive them. We encountered the first locks we had seen since we began our modest walk. A cricket field had a pavilion on which were painted some memorable letters – MCC. This was not the northern headquarters of *the* MCC but the Mytholmroyd Cricket Club. We passed a canalside holiday cottage to let – 'sleeps four and baby' – and Walkley's clog factory. We diverted to walk the platforms of a restored Hebden Bridge railway station.

At the Hebden Bridge Marina, we ate our butties in the sunshine, watching the motorised barge *Gracie Fields* arrive with a load of schoolchildren who were singing 'What Shall we do with a Grumpy Teacher' to the tune 'Drunken Sailor'. A Huddersfield man who was here for the day told me a story of old Huddersfield. It seems that Dick Bell used to sell fish from door to door. Folk said he was daft. He were noan soa daft as he looked. When a customer said the fish she had bought was not fresh, Dick shrugged his shoulders and replied: 'Yo' should hev takken it when Ah offered it t'week afore.'

The manufacturers throve mightily and had big houses built in select parts of town. An architect who told a client about Aspect was asked if a house needed one. On being assured it did, he insisted that if his fellow manufacturers had an aspect, he would like three!

The mill-towns have been transformed. Now we are linked with Europe. When an old lady in Keighley was asked her views on the Common Market, she said: 'I'm moan so bothered what kind o' market it is, as long as its getten a roof on it.'

11   The Deep South

Castleford lasses may weel bi fair,
For they wesh i' t'Calder an' sind i' t'Aire
[Old couplet.]

Seen from the east, the cooling-towers of power stations near the Great North Road are like enormous milk bottles left on the doorstep of Yorkshire. Until recently, the South Yorkshire skyline was also decked with the winding gear at collieries and by mini-mountains of almost unscalable slag. The few remaining deep mines appear to be showing a profit. Much coal is being grabbed from the surface, with the operators creating holes which must be visible from outer space. This part of Yorkshire is not all muck, and it is certainly not all money, but it can produce joyful surprises as well as shocks.

History refuses to lie down at Castleford, where Roman remains were found, and at Roche Abbey where monks tried to live quiet lives. Walter Scott, visiting Conisborough Castle (which has one of the finest remaining Norman keeps in the land), was given a burst of fresh inspiration when writing *Ivanhoe*.

A free-range population of red deer inhabits woodland in part of the old Wharncliffe Chase, where in 1510 Sir Thomas Wortley built a lodge 'that he might hear the hart bel in the midst of Wharncliffe'. The roe deer has returned to the area. A footloose buck was seen swimming a canal. Another trailblazer appeared on the sports field of a school at Knottingley. Before long, the ghost of Robin Hood (who as an outlaw frequented the woods of Barnsdale, South Yorkshire) will be reported from his old haunts, along with the ghostly form of an American film director waving a spectral cheque book.

As for stately homes, Cannon Hall near Barnsley has a superb parkland setting. Wentworth Woodhouse, on the fringe of Rotherham, possesses the longest façade (some six hundred feet) of any private house in England. Sheffield's Meadowcroft shopping centre is one of Europe's largest. The racecourse at Doncaster, one of the oldest, features the St Leger in its Race Week. A new vicar in the district who asked one of his parishioners if he could find a nice treble was himself queried: 'What sort o' treble? Choir or horse-racing?'

You must have heard of Pontefract cakes, which are made of liquorice. This old town is the centre of a major liquorice-growing area. It is grown out of doors, but in long, low, dark sheds northwards towards Leeds, rhubarb is 'brought on' and sent to market early in the season to claim the best prices. The discovery that rhubarb could be 'forced' on a commercial scale was made about the middle of the nineteenth century.

Rhubarb was a traditional garden crop, of course, and it was already known to domestic gardeners that if you put an old bucket over a clump to keep out the sunlight the rhubarb would develop growing pains and not lose any of its sweetness. Furthermore, there was nothing like half a bucket of horse manure to get the stuff moving – and to give it a bit o' flavour.

In the heyday of the industry, when the main strains of rhubarb had patriotic names – Victoria and Prince Albert – the rhubarb-forcing industry extended over a total of about 5,000 acres, calling for enough custard to fill a reservoir. The busy time for the Yorkshire rhubarb growers was during the first three months of the year. Those who 'pulled' the rhubarb did so by the light of candles placed on long rods. A special train conveyed rhubarb to Covent Garden market.

I've met some kindly folk in South Yorkshire. One of them had become a centenarian. A local reporter who visited him said to a neighbour: 'You must be proud of him.' The reply was: 'Ah suppose so. But all he seems to hev done is grow old. He's takken a long time to do that.' An old lady who had (with great difficulty) used a public telephone for the first time was so impressed by the help given by the operator at the exchange she rang her again and remarked: 'Sorry I've given you so much trouble. I'm putting another coin in the machine and it's just for you.'

Life was grim but humour bubbled up. A visitor to Sheffield who saw a dog wearing brown boots asked the owner why this should be. And the owner replied: 'I've takken his black boots to be mended.' A miner's wife was heard shouting to one of her offspring: 'You've brokken yer dad's saucer. Nah what's he bahn to drink his tea out of?'

The village craftsman survives – with an effort. A Londoner stood watching a smith at work. He was delighted to see this demonstration of true craftsmanship. He (the Londoner) was a craftsman. Back at work, he operated to an accuracy of 1/10,000th of an inch. The smith observed, wrily: 'Thee stay and watch me. I'se exact!' It was in a Yorkshire police magazine that I read the pleasant little tale of an old lady who asked a constable if he could see her over the road. He replied: 'Just a tick. I'll nip across and have a look.'

It's a pity that those who enter Yorkshire by train from the south pass through t'muckiest parts of the county on their way from Sheffield to Leeds. Or, conversely, from Leeds to Sheffield. It was the same in the 1830s, when William Cobbett, during one of his 'rural rides' (on horse-back) observed:

All the way from Leeds to Sheffield it is coal and iron and iron and coal. It was dark before we reached Sheffield, so that we saw the iron furnaces in all the horrible splendour of their everlasting blaze ... As to the land, viewed in the way of agriculture, it really does appear to be very little worth. I have not seen, except at Harewood and Ripley, a stack of wheat since I came into Yorkshire.

It cannot have been as bad as all that. Much attractive open country existed in Cobbett's day; and much remains. Woods contain a natural mix of deciduous trees as well as badgers and deer. As the South Yorkshire year advances, cows graze up to their hocks in good grass. It is good poaching country. A man who filled his larder with his Lordship's game was brought before the magistrates and said: 'As God's my judge, I'm innocent.' The chairman declared: 'He isn't. I am. You aren't ...'

The old landed gentry and the local miners had an uneasy relationship. An exception was a man of influence and property who was out riding in his park one morning when he saw an old miner peering between the bars of the main gate. He asked: 'What are you doing, my good man?'

Said the old miner: 'I'm just admiring my estate.'

The landowner snorted and remarked: 'It is my estate.'

The miner remarked: 'Perhaps, but all you can do is look at it. That's what I'm doing now.' The two men relaxed. Affability prevailed. The miner invited the landowner to visit his estate, which he did. They stood in the tiny backyard of a terraced house.

Said the landowner: 'Your estate is not very big.'

The miner replied: 'Appen not – but look up. See how high it is!'

Brierley and Frickley are pit names which bely their ugly nature. Grimeworth, an ancient name, foretold the future state of the district. Ackworth, where the men 'addled' brass more from quarrying than mining, is still an attractive place, with a distinguished Friends' School and the stately pile of Nostell Priory, where his lordship drew money from coal pits and brickworks, while maintaining a pleasant view from his home of a tract of parkland and cornfield.

Lord St Oswald's estate was frequently 'open to view' and you had to enter his hallowed acres via the main gates to attend services at Wragby Church. On Hospital Sunday, a grand-stand was erected and local churches combined to sing hymns. The Conservatives had their fetes in the priory grounds. One year, locals were shocked when all-in wrestling was introduced. Two young teachers, recently married, met a local headmaster who did not think that wrestling was suitable for an innocent young lady. He insisted on the couple leaving the park.

Some villages, built on (and of) magnesium limestone, look half as old as time. A mining village like Upton is most attractive in summer, especially now that the colliery has been closed. The red of massed brick, from house and bungalow, contrast vividly with the gold of corn stubble. At one of the old colliery villages, they tell the story of a redundant man who applied for a job and was told: 'We've nothing for you. We're quite full up.' He said that surely there was a job of some sort for him. The foreman said: 'Nay – we've a man for every job in the place.' The redundant man pleaded to be given work, adding: 'The little bit I did wouldn't make much difference.'

Spirits were kept up by the local brass bands, which are among the finest in the land. The conductor of one band gave a trumpet-player a chance to join but after the first few bars had been played he yelled: 'Tha's two bars behind the others.' The man on probation said: 'Aye, I know. Don't worry. I can catch t'others up any time I want to.'

Generally, South Yorkshire is a brighter, cleaner area than it was. There are pollutants, however. The Great North Road, a major artery, was once a highway of romance – a setting for outlaws clad in Lincoln green, horse-drawn coaches, highwaymen, eloping couples and pedlars. Today, a sensible chicken would not even contemplate crossing the road; it would try to find an underpass or a bridge. A small boy, instilling kerb drill into his pal, said: 'Look out – or thou'll finish up as potted meat.'

Crossing this major road is an east-west motorway, linking Hull and Manchester. As I write, there are proposals for a massive opencast coal site near Wakefield. A local councillor commented: 'What we don't want is to see the scars of our mining past – which are now healing, with cattle grazing on them – ripped apart once again with no real benefit for our communities.'

My first acquaintance with South Yorkshire came when an aunt and uncle lived at Rotherham. Molly was a Skipton lass who married Uncle Harold. He was something in the steel industry at Sheffield. In their day, Rotherham and adjacent Sheffield lay under an almost permanent pall of industrial smoke. It was said that when a Rotherham lass first visited the country, she was anxious not to show complete ignorance of country ways. A dish of honey was set before her at breakfast time. She looked delighted and said: 'I'm glad to see you keep a bee.'

Their part of Rotherham was hardly typical. Not a single factory or steelworks was in view. Instead, their semi-detached house stood in a single street, at the end of which stood Keppel's Column, a lofty pillar raised in honour of Admiral Keppel, following his honourable acquittal at a court martial following the Battle of Brest in 1778. The view took in the rolling acres extending to Wentworth Woodhouse, a mansion which (as I have already mentioned) has a 600-foot frontage.

This huge building had a setting to match its grandeur, presiding over a 1,500-acre park. The estate passed from the Wentworths to the Rockinghams and the Fitzwilliams, which meant 400 years of habitation by families with close ties either through descent or marriage. When I first strode beside the façade of what its builder described as 'stupendous architecture', some ninety rooms were being used by the Lady Mabel College of Education. Which reminds me of the response of a Yorkshire lad to his teacher, when she quoted: 'I come to bury Caesar, not to praise him' and invited the lad to tell her who had said it. He thought for a moment, then replied: 'It must have been the undertaker.'

A glimpse of majestic Wentworth Woodhouse is a reminder of the South Yorkshire that was. Sheffield is believed to have taken its name from 'open land by the Sheaf', one of the five local rivers. The old Sheffield was mentioned by Chaucer in *The Canterbury Tales*, where the miller of Trumpington carried 'in his hose' a 'Sheffield thwitel' or knife. The place was renowned for its knives, sickles, shears and similar products, many of which were made from ironstone mined in the nearby hills, using grindstones quarried locally.

The Cutler's Company of Hallamshire was created in 1624 and part of the décor of the Cutlers' Hall are words written by John Ruskin, who at another time referred to Sheffield as 'a dark picture in a golden frame'. The city had become the premier place in the British steel industry following the experiments of Benjamin Huntsman, who early in the eighteenth century melted scraps of bar steel until, to quote Samuel Smiles, it had 'a clear surface of a dazzling brilliancy like the sun when looked at with the naked eye on a clear day'. This crucible steel was then cast into simple shapes for forging. It could be produced uniformly and of high quality.

Sheffield is in Yorkshire – but nobbut just. Because it has a border situation, it stresses its Yorkshireness and is proud of its early connections with Yorkshire cricket, the old Darnall ground at Sheffield being (in 1825) the venue of the first representative game, a 22 of Yorkshire against England. Yorkshire lost by only twenty-eight runs. The event caused great excitement, the streets of Sheffield being full of 'pedestrians, gigs and waterloos'.

Tom Marsden, one of the early cricketers, was a left-hand batsman as well as a devastatingly fast underarm bowler. At Bramall Lane, Sheffield, two Essex men were resisting the efforts of the home bowlers for hours. A doleful Yorkshire spectator said: 'I'd rather fish in a pool where there's no fish na watch them two lads bat.' Once, when Neville Cardus watched Yorkshire play, the crowd roared 'Owzat?' Involuntarily, Cardus expressed a contrary opinion. A Yorkshire spectator eyed him from boots to crown, then slowly remarked: 'And what's the matter wi' thee?'

South Yorkshire is the region of Dearne and Don and Aire, which rise in the Pennines as gushing watercourses and pick up life-snuffing doses of pollution on the way. Sooner or later, you'll encounter Barnsley. It now signifies coil (coal), yet this was for many years – as its name, a barn in a clearing, implies – a quiet farming community, surrounded by fields and woods. Barnsley became a market town in 1249 when a grant was made by Henry II to the monks of St John's, Pontefract.

Penistone, high on the Pennines, had engineering grafted on to farming and blossomed accordingly at 225 metres above sea level. Cawthorne is one of the prettiest villages in Yorkshire. So is Silkstone, which named a seam of coal. The core of the village is old; the place has, in recent years, become cocooned by modern housing.

South Yorkshire has its great medieval themes, none more alluring than the legends of Robin Hood, who as related frequented the glades of Barnsdale. Forget the Hollywood treatment, in which Robin and his men lived in the Greenwood with a hundred-piece orchestra and the dishy Maid Marion (who, in truth, was a French lass, introduced to the tales later to give them a bit of glamour). How on earth did they all manage to live in a wet and mossy wood and stay so clean and tidy? A major tourist attraction in old Sherwood is insulated from wind and weather by transparent material.

Robert de Hode was a Wakefield lad. He and his merrie (drunken?) men are said to have robbed the rich to help the poor. If he was a Yorkshireman, he would hope to do better than just break even! They do say that Robin Hood died a luvly death at Kirkless, near Brighouse. A snag occurred when they dug at the reputed spot and found the earth had not been disturbed.

The coal industry transformed the district. The tilt of the land meant that coal had been found high on the western hills but was deep below ground in the east. Early pits were sunk around Leeds and Bradford. The deeper seams had to await the evolution of industrial know-how. Old Pontefract was built on coal. Many years ago, when the borough council demolished some old and decayed property near the castle, and gaps appeared at the centre of the town, the redevelopers found a pillar of coal, providing a site of greater stability than anywhere else in the district. On part of that land, some multi-storey blocks of flats were built.

Pontefract once found employment for 4,000 coal miners, a quarter of the insured population, yet in a part of Yorkshire where red bricks are numbered in trillions, the place had retained a pleasant profusion of greystone buildings. Black was Pontefract's favourite colour (if one accepts black as a colour rather than a total absence of it). Here is to be found the juicy black of a confection called liquorice. Ten factories were once devoted to producing liquorice products, such as Pontefract (or Pomfret) cakes. The familiar black discs had the impression of the local castle gateway stamped on them.

Collieries were to be found near Merrie Wakefield (thus called, it is theorised, because of the number of pubs). Doncaster, a market town since Roman times, and having a large and varied collection of grants and charters, was a coaching place on the Great North Road, a place where every other person made butterscotch and the remainder of the workforce was employed on the railway – or so I have been told.

Mining has had instances of grim humour. There was nowt funny in groping about for coil in t'bowels of the earth. One tale I heard in the mining area still makes me wince. A visitor to a pub saw a man who was only four feet high and with a cauliflower ear. He was said to have stood six feet high before an emergency in the mine when, heroically, as the roof was about to collapse, he volunteered to support it while his friends got clear. The stranger, impressed, commented on the cauliflower ear and was told: 'We had to knock him into position.'

At a café in Barnsley, a dear old lady was sitting at the same table as a burly man. She asked him if he could pass her the sugar basin.

He replied: 'Ah reckon so, luv. I've spent most of my life shifting ruddy coal.'

The mining communities of South Yorkshire included Hemsworth, where three phases of house construction are evident. Local brick, with slate roofs, mark the turn-of-the-century building. The council houses of the 1930s are distinctive and so are the post-1945 bungaloid development at the fringes of town. I suppose there are the usual instances of jerry-building, such as when the builder invited a prospective buyer to go into the next room and then whispered: 'Can you hear me?' 'Yes.'

The despairing builder said: 'Can you see me?' 'No.' The builder said with forced enthusiasm: 'There's a fine house for you!'

Hemsworth was spoken of as a 'bread and herring' pit, where there was a lot of work for little pay. Now there's – nowt! The pit headgear, buildings and waste stacks have gone, leaving (when I last saw it) a broad grassy plain. The palatial working men's club (with one thousand members) has survived in good shape. A typical 'new' colliery village, constructed at the turn of the century, was run on a strict system relating to colliery status. A posh house was earmarked for the manager. An official had a house in which the front door opened into a passage, and not directly into the cramped living room, as was the case with the dwellings of miners.

Free coal kept the houses hot. Dumped beside the house at the rate of a ton a month, it enabled some families to keep two fires burning the year through. In hot weather, it was like living in a kiln. A fire was 'built up with slack' as the last person prepared for work. Next morning, the fire was broddled (stirred up with a poker). Broddle was also a term used for ensuring the tea was well-brewed. (In other parts of Yorkshire, the word was 'mashed'.)

After the warm conditions underground, heat was as important to the miner as food. He must have a big fire. The poky living room had a table, chairs (including a rocker), mangle and set-pot (to be used for the clothes on washing day). The working man's house had a tiny pantry and a glory hole (lobby). The miners were hard workers and hard drinkers. Many showed by their corpulence the effects of excessive eating and too much strong drink. The women spent most of their time at home, doing housework and raising children.

Colliery villages waxed and waned with the fortunes of mining. When times were good, workers and their families were sucked in from distant places. Upton was an interesting case because after a labour force had been housed locally a geological fault led to the closures of the colliery. The families drifted away. As someone lamented: 'If there were many more few of us, there wouldn't be enough.' The mining families returned when the geological problem had been overcome.

Old folk have childhood memories of the days before pithead baths were installed. Miners who returned home after work were in their 'pit muck', being black and grimy with coal dust. A miner went to the sink, where there was just a cold water tap. He washed his hands and forearms before sitting at a plain deal table to eat his first substantial meal of the day. On pay-day, his plate was heaped with the left-overs of previous meals, followed by rice puddings and a pint pot of tea.

Then he would sit back, still in his dirty clothes, and read the newspaper, studying form and updating himself on the state of football. Before he went to bed, he would wash his face and chest, but otherwise he was nearly as black as the coal. It was a matter of 'legs once a week, back once a week.' Now and again, the miner sat in the soapy swell within a zinc bath set before the fire. When, in due course, the council got round to providing houses with bathrooms, tales began to circulate of miners keeping part of their supply of free coal in the bath.

Miners augmented the domestic fuel supply by the produce of their allotments. During one strike, vegetables were being stolen at night. Some of the allotment-holders lay in wait and as the thieves appeared they slipped white sheets over their heads and howled like banshees. The intruders fled.

Life was cheap. One might even laugh at death. A mining widow related: 'He went out for some stewing steak and dropped down dead.'

Her friend, greatly concerned, said: 'What on earth did you do?'

The new widow said, quietly: 'I had to open a tin of corned beef.'

When he heard Owd Jack had died, aged ninety-two, a miner inquired the cause of death. He was told: 'Ah've no idea – but it were summat quite serious.'

And there's an old, old tale about a miner and his wife who were discussing the future. She said: 'If owt 'appens to me, I'd not mind you getting wed again, only I wouldn't like to think she was wearing my clothes.'

He replied: 'Don't worry, lass. She's tried 'em on. They don't fit her.'

The old Norse name leika, which became the Yorkshire laik, meaning 'to play', was ironic in the 1930s, when the pits were closed and out-of-work miners wiled away their daytimes at street corners and on waste land. They scrabbled about on the slagheaps, looking for bits of coal. It could be a dangerous occupation. Slagheaps smouldered and occasionally burst into flames.

The mining community was noted for the decorative effect of brightly scoured doorsteps and window-sills. The old-time miner had his whippets and his pigeons. There was a love of pageantry once a year when a miners' gala filled the streets with bands, marching men and colourful banners.

The council schools provided remarkably good education and at Upton, twice a week in the 1930s, the children had a special midday treat – fish and chips. Orders were taken and money collected. At 11-30, two fish and chip monitors bore a large clothes basket to the shop, returning with the food, plus a bottle of vinegar and some salt. At school, the tables were decked with flowers and set out with warmed plates and cutlery. A waste-paper basket was provided for the discarded, greasy paper.

The miners were determined men. I met a retired and crippled man as he walked slowly up a hill with the aid of two sticks. He said: 'T'doctor wanted me to have a wheelchair. I telled him he could keep it. I'll walk as long as I can.'

Hoyland, a hill town between Barnsley and Sheffield, sprang into industrial prominence mainly through mining. Its good fortune was that it lay near seams of quality coal – enough coal to keep a ring of collieries busy. At Hoyland, the New Year was welcomed not only by the sweet sound of church bells but by the wailing of colliery buzzers. On the stroke of midnight there was a veritable chorus – and of such disharmony it portended much of modern music. (At a South Yorkshire cafe, when a waitress dropped a tray, three couples got up to dance). The New Year buzz stopped at the beginning of the 1939–45 war and was not resumed.

At Nostell, near Wakefield, the six o'clock buzzer was prolonged if no miners were required at the pit on the following day. An especially long blast, rather like an air-raid warning, meant there had been an accident. A quick hoot meant that the buzzer-man had tripped.

Who would have thought that Yorkshire's coal-mining industry would have declined so quickly from its peak when, in an area of eight hundred square miles, there were about 125,000 miners with a potential production of fifty million tons a year? Or that under privatisation, people were talking of each of the remaining miners in deep pits earning £30,000 a year? Now the heady rush to cash in on rich seams of coal has taken a new turn. Many pits have been closed down and the land round about re-instated. Colliery villages scarcely had time to develop traditions. The South Yorkshire speech – with its clipped words, short a's and a dropping of aitches – has something of the quality of the native tongue in a D.H. Lawrence novel.

The modern threat to South Yorkshire is from opencast mining, near Barnsley and extending towards Doncaster, Pontefract, Wakefield – even Leeds and Bradford. A local MP, commenting on an area which having done its bit had become a lake, popular with local fishermen, commented: 'We are people who live in

former pit villages linked by small pockets of green space which
provide our recreation. Why should we have these areas taken
away by opencast developers seeking to open them up again?
Several years ago, people lost their jobs and homes because they
were told no one wanted the coal.'

As I read this, I thought I heard a chuckle. Could it have been
an old miner, now living in a celestial village, who had just said to
himself: 'Nowt changes'. At Tankersley churchyard, which lies
near the motorway, a lady who was putting flowers on the grave of
a loved one said: 'I don't know how the dead manage to sleep. The
traffic noises must be very trying for them.'

12 Ouse and Humber

Lincoln was, London is, but York shall be
The greatest city of the three.
[Traditional couplet.]

York, in medieval times, would appear like a mirage from the central plain of Yorkshire – the low ground, dating back to the melting of glacial ice and the deposition of a layer of boulder clay, which divides Yorkshire into two halves, providing a geographical interlude between the Pennines and the North-east Moors.

Gleaming limestone formed the defensive walls, which were pierced by four bars, or gates. The grey rock, stacked on rafts and floated down the Ouse from Tadcaster was landed near the Guildhall and hauled by sled to where it was needed for the construction of the Minster, one of the most impressive buildings in England. The city walls of York, standing on grassed-over banks, are in early spring bright with daffodils. The walls were said to keep unfriendly people out, but in a discussion between a York man and a friend who lived in Lancaster, when talk drifted to the subject of lunatic asylums, the York man asked, teasingly: 'Is it right that there were seven lunatic asylums in Lancaster?'

Said the man from Lancaster: 'Appen so. But remember – they'd to build a ruddy wall all round York!'

The walls ensured that from the dawn of the fourteenth century until the seventeenth-century York remained a compact city. Almost forty years ago, when the city planning officer, Charles Minter and his staff prepared a development survey, they commented that as a result of this growth behind the walls – which meant continual building and rebuilding – there developed the

153

present congested narrow streets and picturesque medley of buildings of every architectural style from the Middle Ages to the present day.

I visited Charles Minter when some of the city bars (gates) were being restored. He had invited me to address a gathering at the Methodist church and I was offered overnight accommodation. For hours, until almost midnight, we exchanged Yorkshire stories, such as that of the cricket match at a village near York where the opening batsman snicked the ball into the stumper's hands. The cry of 'owzat' was ignored by the umpire, but the batsman, troubled, later went up to him and said: 'I did hit that ball.' The umpire agreed but added: 'It were nobbut slight.'

York stands on a triangular stretch of flat land formed by the junction of the Fosse and Ouse. The city has an uneasy relationship with the Ouse, which is part of Yorkshire's main drain. When there's heavy rain and a sudden thaw of snow lying on the Pennines, the Ouse gets middle-aged spread and householders threatened with inundation tap their barometers with all the gusto of woodpeckers at their nesting trees. One man, seeing the instrument was stubbornly set 'fair', when outdoors the rain continued, took it into the yard, held it up and cried: 'Sitha!' This, translated into standard English, means 'have a look'.

Winter at York may be cheerless, with fog. This sends the temperature plunging and it prompted a woman to visit a chemist's shop for a thermometer. She picked one up, handed it to the assistant, and said: 'I'll take this Fahrenheit one. I know it's a good brand.'

Gruesome tales are to be heard at York, including public hangings at York Castle. It is said that when the last took place, a villager walked eleven miles into the city to observe it. The victim was dispatched. A woman wailed. The visitor said: 'At least he's escaped from this wicked world. I've got to walk eleven miles home again – and these new shoes are nearly killing me!'

The jumble of buildings at the medieval core of the city is criss-crossed by 'a human rabbit warren' of snicket, ginnels and alleys. Mark W. Jones devised a walk around these 'snickle-ways' and in the accompanying booklet has some amusing comments to make, even about litter.

Disgraceful though this is, and an indictment of our English litterloutishness, it is as much in keeping with the past as the ancient paving-slabs. The beer cans and fish-and-chip wrappings are the modern equivalent of the noisome rubbish deposited in these alleys by our forebears, who left bones, offal and other unspeakable garbage to accumulate. But they had no disposal service. We have no excuse.

The three major tourist attractions at York – Minster, Railway Museum and Coppergate (a novel introduction to the place as it was in Viking days) – ensure that the medieval bustle in the narrow streets continues to this day.

Standing at the northern end of the Plain of York are four towns where it is easily possible to evoke the coaching era. I refer to Northallerton, Thirsk, Boroughbridge and Ripon, each with its coaching inns and, in the case of Thirsk and Ripon, capacious market-places. Northallerton was the birthplace of the forthright John Radcliffe. He became a doctor and, called upon for medical advice by Queen Anne, told her straight – there was nowt wrong with her!

Thirsk has a long history but will be forever associated with a man who lived in recent times. Alf Wight, who was born in Weardale and spent his early life in Glasgow, became a vet at Thirsk and, writing under the pen-name James Herriot, produced many charming books about the Dales. He related to me some of his Dales experiences. I told him the story of a lady who had just returned home after the funeral of her husband, a funeral which was followed by the customary tea at a local hotel. She told a neighbour: "'E 'edn't bin a gooid 'usband, but I put him away nicely wi' two sooarts o' meight [meat].'

Thirsk, an endearing spot, includes among its modern characters the astonishing William Foggitt, who has achieved national renown as a weather forecaster. Every morning he takes note of the wind speed and direction. In the absence of a weather vane at his home, South Villa, he reaches for binoculars and consults the vane on the church tower at Thirsk. His long-range forecasts are based on a consultation of records kept by the Foggitt family over many years.

A journalist rang him about the middle of January, when the weather was severe, asking how long the cold snap was going to last. Bill looked at the barometer, which was falling. He had just noticed that moles were 'starting up' and he said: 'Oh! There'll be a thaw.' The journalist asked him when this was likely to be. Bill

Foggitt thought he would not rush it and said: 'Thursday'. That was the day the meteorologists brought into service a new computer and they forecast a blizzard. Instead, there was a thaw, as Bill had foretold. His fame spread. A reporter working on a brash tabloid newspaper rang him up for some observations about the weather and Bill said: 'The cuckoo is silent. That shows it's pretty cold.' Next morning, a bold headline proclaimed: SILENT CUCKOO TELLS ALL!

Ripon is a small city which has virtually every desirable feature, even a little racecourse. A former dean of Ripon (the Very Revd F.L. Hughes) was dining in London when an Italian waiter asked him where he lived and went into ecstasies at the reply. 'Ripon!' he exclaimed. 'That's the place with a nice little racecourse.' When can you consider yourself a native of the place? A variation on the Thirsk tale of a funeral tea is an account of a man who, while coming away from a funeral, said to a friend that the deceased, who had lived in the place for seventy years, was an old Riponian. His companion said: 'No he weren't. His mother came from 'Elperby and he's got no one in t'churchyard.'

At the source of the Ouse, the most powerful of the Yorkshire rivers, there is not a drop of water in sight. A stone pillar with the inscription Ouse Head stands in the grounds of a former workhouse, now used by corn and seed merchants, not far from the splendidly named Great Ouseburn. When a water diviner surveyed Ouse Head, he felt the rod twitching in his hand at a distance of five or six yards from the pillar. In the next field are some springs and, near a hedge, the Ousegill Beck appears, hastening to the Ure, which had already absorbed the Swale.

The Ouse begins modestly with Ouse Gill Beck. Near where the waters meet there was a signpost with two arms – one indicating the Ure and the other, pointing downriver, identifying the Ouse. Aldwark, a village on the Plain, would scarcely be known to outsiders were it not for its toll bridge. The toll house has white exterior walls and red pantiles on the roof. Long before the bridge was constructed, ferries were used at this river crossing point. The Roman landing-stage was discovered in recent times.

The first wooden bridge collapsed one winter in the middle of the last century. Icefloes were being carried along by the water. Fourteen children, fascinated by the sight, were on the bridge when it tumbled and they were thrown into the water. All but one of them died. In a serious flood, a quarter of a century ago, a her hut floated downriver. A cockerel, perched on the hut, crowed loudly until the hut, swept clear of the bridge supports, sank in the deeps beyond. The cockerel was presumed drowned.

There has been traffic on the Ouse at Cawood throughout recorded history. The Romans sailed the river in gilded barges. Vikings, using long boats with dragonesque prows and striped sails, used the Ouse to penetrate deeply into Yorkshire. It was at Cawood that I heard a Norse story with a difference. Two men were talking. One said he was sure his wife had Viking blood. Why? 'She eats like an 'orse.'

Cawood's farm-hands, working long hours, developed healthy appetites which were not always satisfied. A hired man who, hired at Martinmas, lived in with the family, was in a field manuring potato rows prior to the potatoes being set when his boss told him to use plenty of manure because 'tatties are hungry things'. The disgruntled farm-hand replied: 'So I see. At dinner-time, when we had meat pie, my tatties had eaten up most o' t'meat.'

In the days before coaches provided mobility for poorer folk, villagers at Cawood were in the habit, in their spare time, of standing at the edge of the Ouse, discussing the affairs of the day and meanwhile gazing at the opposite bank of the river. Then came the day when Cawood had a trip to Scarborough by coach. Several of the old friends stood gazing out to sea. One man expressed what was in every mind: 'By gor, lads, she's a hell of a width.'

The folk living south of the Ouse have not had many links with adjacent areas. They lived on what became known as the Isle of Axholme. It formed a little country on its own. Here was the top corner of a former great fen which once stretched unbroken down through Cambridgeshire into East Anglia. The residents used the reeds to thatch their homes. They augmented their food by slaughtering waterfowl. At certain times of year, the air was blackened by ducks and geese.

Drained by the industrious Dutch, the fen is now a tract of top-quality arable land. The rustle of reeds has given way to the rustle of wheat stalks. The villages have enchanting names – Swinefleet, Reedness, Whitgift, Ousefleet. The mighty Ouse has had its course altered and its edges banked up. The village of Blacktoft lies east of Goole and to the north of the river, yet Blacktoft Sands (a famous nature reserve) are on t'other side, a consequence of a river-training wall constructed in the 1920s.

Blacktoft Sands are at the confluence of Ouse and Trent, below which lies the port of Goole and the broad sweep of the Humber estuary, which has a watershed nearly one-fifth the land surface of England. From the mile-long span of the stupendous Humber Bridge, which was opened in 1981, a visitor can look down for 512 feet on a waste of khaki-coloured water, a veritable battleground of river and tide. Yorkshire pride is manifest in the Humber Bridge, though some call it a 'white elephant'. In mid-1995, it was still the world's longest span.

Hull is the salt-water city, where I have stared open mouthed as a huge ferry has entered its dock with the best part of a foot to spare on either side – or so it seemed. The Queen's Dock was filled in, converted into gardens, with artificial ponds complete with goldfish, if the gulls have left any. Children are not seen playing in the street as they used to do before toy firms and television cashed in on their play time. A Hull lady, hurrying home, overtook a procession of small children. She spoke to the leading boy, who was pulling a pram, but was 'shushed', for this (he said) was a funeral. The lady persisted, asking whose funeral it was, whereupon the lad said, gruffly: 'How the heck do I know. I'm t'oss [horse].'

At Hull I heard of the Salvation Army bandsman who, at an interlude during an impromptu out-of-doors meeting, slipped down a ginnel to have a smoke. He was spotted and told that if God had intended him to smoke, he would have fitted a chimney to the top of his head. The unrepentant bandsman said: 'And if we were meant to blow gurt brass instruments, He'd have fitted us wi' bellows.' At a local band concert, the trombone player asked his neighbour for the name of the next piece and was told: 'It'll be Handel's Largo.' The trombone player smiled and said: 'I've just played that!'

It has been estimated that at any particular time there are 1.25 million tons of silt in suspension in the Humber. In Roman times, it was virtually a sea, spreading far inland. The warp deposited enriched the soil. A vast area of land was reclaimed by Dutch engineers. In 1797, a survey was made from Spurn Head to Sunk Island in the Lower Humber by William Bligh, who would achieve fame as the captain of *The Bounty*.

This part of Yorkshire is a vast farmscape, with a few villages and farms to break up the scene. At one farm I heard a poem about a small boy which someone had memorised from eighty years before:

> He dried up his tears,
> On his little white brat (apron),
> And tried to say summat,
> Ah cudna tell what.
> His little face breetened,
> Wi' pleasure all through,
> It's right cappin' sometimes,
> What a 'awpenny (halfpenny) will do.

Three thousand years ago, Bronze Age man crossed the Humber on vessels built of oak timbers. A thousand years later, the Romans had their 'great ferry', using a ship with three banks of oars. Before the Humber Bridge was built, the ferry service was maintained (subject to disruption by low tides and shifting sandbanks) in car-carrying paddle steamers.

The river folk are more sophisticated than they were. Many years ago, a smart motor vessel entered the Humber and passed an ancient sailing ship which was laden with coal. The captain of the motor vessel hailed a man on the deck of the collier and asked why he was flying the black flag. The shouted reply was: 'Doan't let our captain hear you say that. It's his shirt.'

Yorkshire ends where the North Sea and the Humber fight it out, in a flurry of khaki-tinted water, off Spurn Point, an unstable peninsula, which someone compared with a tear-drop falling off the face of the county.

Let Florence Hopper, who used to live at Driffield, on the Wolds, have the last words:

> An' as t'sun sinks owerd hill,
> So ends me teeal [tale].
> Another day's come an' gone.
> An' we've all done weeal [well].